M000285005

The Best of
F.B.
MEYER

HONOR
CLASSICS

The Best of

F.B. MEYER

120 DAILY DEVOTIONS
to NURTURE YOUR SPIRIT *and*
REFRESH YOUR SOUL

Edited and Compiled by Stephen W. Sorenson

HONOR **HB** BOOKS
Inspiration and Motivation for the Seasons of Life

COOK COMMUNICATIONS MINISTRIES
Colorado Springs, Colorado • Paris, Ontario
KINGSWAY COMMUNICATIONS LTD
Eastbourne, England

Honor® is an imprint of
Cook Communications Ministries, Colorado Springs, CO 80918
Cook Communications, Paris, Ontario
Kingsway Communications, Eastbourne, England

THE BEST OF F. B. Meyer
© 2006 by Cook Communications Ministries

All rights reserved. No part of this book may be reproduced without
written permission, except for brief quotations in books and critical
reviews. For information, write Cook Communications Ministries, 4050
Lee Vance View, Colorado Springs, CO 80918.

Cover Design: Jackson Design CO, LLC/Greg Jackson

First Printing, 2006
Printed in the United States of America

1 2 3 4 5 6 7 8 9 10 Printing/Year 10 09 08 07 06

All Scripture quotations are taken from the New King James Version.
Copyright © 1982 by Thomas Nelson, Inc. Used by permission. All rights
reserved.

Editor's note: The selections in this book have been "gently modern-
ized" for today's reader. Words, phrases, and sentence structure have
been updated for readability and clarity; new chapter headings and
Scripture verses have been combined with excerpts from F. B. Meyer's
text. Every effort has been made to preserve the integrity and intent of
Meyer's original writings. Reflection questions at the end of each reading have been included to aid in personal exploration and group
discussion.

ISBN-13: 978-1-56292-581-9
ISBN-10: 1-56292-581-4

LCCN: 2005938413

He Preached As If He Had Seen God Face-to-Face

———

M ake the most of me that can be made for Thy glory."
That was the life motto of Frederick Brotherton (F. B.)
Meyer, one of the most influential and beloved preachers of
the late 1800s and early 1900s. A Baptist pastor, author, evangelist, and social reformer, Meyer helped to shape much of the
Christian thought and practice of his day—while leading thousands to Christ through his writings and evangelistic crusades.

Born in 1847 and raised in a Christian home, Meyer bene-
fited from an upbringing that nurtured his faith and nourished
his mind. He went on to graduate from London University in
1869, followed by theological training at Regents Park Baptist
College. In 1872, Dr. Meyer became pastor of Priory Street
Baptist Chapel, where he met the American evangelist D. L.
Moody. These two godly men formed a lifelong friendship, and
for decades they would challenge, encourage, and inspire each
other in the faith.

In 1895, Meyer accepted a call to pastor Christ Church in
London, which had only one hundred members at the time.
Within two years, the church had grown to more than two
thousand. Meyer remained at Christ Church for the next fifteen years, after which he began a ministry of conference
preaching and evangelism. Although his work was based in
England, he was a frequent visitor to the United States and

Canada. He also traveled extensively throughout South Africa and the Far East on mission endeavors.

A major theme of Meyer's life—his own spiritual experience and his ministry to others—was the balance between individual holiness and active faith applied in practical ways. While some denominations and Christian movements emphasized one or the other, Meyer strongly believed that Christians should strive for both a deep, consecrated walk with God *and* the expression of commitment to Him through involvement with the world.

As such, Meyer was a key figure in the Keswick Convention, a significant religious movement that began in Britain and spread through many parts of the world. This movement emphasized absolute surrender to God, individual purity, and complete devotion to Christ. Meyer was a frequent speaker at Keswick events and a leader who helped to broaden its reach and effectiveness. He challenged the thousands of people involved in this movement to deepen their relationship with God while actively and practically applying their faith.

As author and historian Ian M. Randall said, "The Keswick message, as Meyer experienced and then shaped it, unified the mystical and the practical elements in his thinking. Keswick Convention audiences identified with Meyer's twin emphases on the steps into deep experience through the Holy Spirit and the outworking of this in the world."[1]

An ardent Baptist, Meyer became personally involved in confronting social problems, such as alcohol abuse, prostitu-

tion, out-of-wedlock births, and many others. He was instru-
mental in a prohibition effort called the Blue Ribbon
Movement; the Purity, Rescue, and Temperance work of the
Central South London Free Church Council, which closed
brothels and counseled prostitutes; and the Homeless
Children's Aid and Adoption Society.

Being active in social reform earned Meyer, not surpris-
ingly, admiration in some quarters and disdain in others. In
1911, for instance, he rallied against prize fighting, which he
considered brutal and inhumane. His efforts resulted in the
cancellation of a much-publicized fight to be held at Earl's
Court between Jack Johnson of the United States and a British
contender. Meyer endured scorn for his efforts, and a London
newspaper called him "Meddling, Maudlin Meyer." A man of
deep conviction and spiritual passion, he did not let public
ridicule deter his reform efforts, and he continued to take on
social causes throughout his life.

In addition to his social-reform efforts, Meyer served as
president of the National and World Sunday School Unions,
president of the National Christian Endeavor, and founder of
South London Missionary Training College. He was the author
of more than forty books, including *The Secret of Guidance* and
The Way into the Holiest.

During his long and fruitful life, Meyer preached more
than sixteen thousand sermons. He had great influence upon
such giants of the faith as J. Wilbur Chapman and Charles
Spurgeon. It was Spurgeon who said, "Meyer preaches as a

man who has seen God face-to-face." At the age of eighty, Meyer conducted his twelfth American preaching campaign, traveling some fifteen thousand miles and speaking at more than three hundred meetings. Meyer returned to England to pastor for several more years before he died in 1929. Few would disagree that his life motto to be used fully for God's glory was indeed fulfilled.

───────◦◦◦◦───────

† Ian M. Randall, "F. B. Meyer: Baptist Ambassador for Keswick Holiness Spirituality," Baptist History and Heritage Society, 2002.

Make Time for Stillness and Solitude with God

———◆◆◆———

*"He who says he abides in Him ought himself also
to walk just as He walked."*

1 JOHN 2:6

When Jesus redeemed us with His blood and presented us to the Father in His righteousness, He did not leave us in our old nature to serve God as best we could. No, in Him dwelled the eternal life, the divine life of heaven. Everyone who is in Him receives from Him that same eternal life in its holy heavenly power. So nothing can be more natural than the claim that the person who abides in Jesus, continually receiving life from Him, must also walk as He walked.

This mighty life of God does not work as a blind force, compelling us ignorantly or involuntarily to act like Christ. On the contrary, walking like Him must come as a result of a deliberate choice, sought in strong desire, accepted by a living will.

When He calls us to abide in Him that we may receive that life more abundantly, He points us to His life on Earth and tells us that the new life has been bestowed so we will walk as He walked. We are to think, speak, and act as Jesus did. As He was, so we are to be.

Reflection
What specifically does it mean to "walk like Christ" in daily
life? How can you more closely follow His example this week?

Abide in Him Always

"One thing I have desired of the LORD, that will I seek: that I may dwell in the house of the LORD all the days of my life."

PSALM 27:4

Every crocus pushing through the dark mold, every firefly in the forest, every bird that springs up from its nest before your feet, everything that is—*all* are as full of God's presence as the bush that burned with His fire, before which Moses bared his feet in acknowledgment that God was there.

But we do not always realize it. We often pass hours, days, and weeks seeking assurance that He is with us. We sometimes engage in seasons of prayer, hoping for a special word from the Lord or touch of His hand. We go from one activity or meeting to another. Still He is a shadow, a name, a tradition, a dream of days gone by.

If only we could feel, as the apostle put it on Mars Hill, that God is not far away. He is with us, near us, and in us always. We should understand what David meant when he spoke about dwelling in the house of the Lord all the days of his life, beholding His beauty, inquiring in His temple, and hiding in the secret of His pavilion (see Psalm 27). Let us endeavor to learn the blessed secret of abiding ever in the secret of His presence and of being hidden in His pavilion.

Reflection

What does it mean to abide in Jesus' presence each day?

3

Seek God's Unerring Guidance

"The LORD will guide you continually."
ISAIAH 58:11

So much of our power and peace consists in knowing where God would have us be—and in just being there. If we are precisely where our heavenly Father wants us, we are perfectly sure that He will provide food and clothes and everything besides. When He sends His servants to Cherith, He will make even the ravens bring them food (see 1 Kings 17:1–6).

How much of our Christian work has been ineffective because we have persisted in initiating it for ourselves instead of ascertaining what God was doing and where He required our presence! We dream bright dreams of success. We try to command it. We call to our aid all kinds of resources, questionable or otherwise. At last we turn back, disheartened and ashamed, like children who are torn and scratched by the brambles and soiled by the quagmire. None of this would have happened if only we had been, from the first, under God's unerring guidance. He might test us, but He could not allow us to err.

Children of God who long to know their Father's will turn to the Bible and gain confidence by noticing how in all ages God has guided those who dared to trust Him completely, even as those same people must have at the time been as perplexed as we often are now. We see how Abraham left all that was familiar and started, with no other guide than God, across the trackless desert to a land he didn't know. We see how for forty years the Israelites were led through the peninsula of Sinai, with its labyrinths of red sandstone and wastes of sand. It is impossible to think that God could guide us at all if He did not guide us always. So we are bidden to look for guidance that will embrace the whole of life in all its myriad necessities.

Reflection

In which areas have you sought your own guidance rather than God's? What happened?

4

Thank God for All Things

———◦◦◦———

3

*"Be filled with the Spirit ... giving thanks always for all things
to God the Father in the name of our Lord Jesus Christ."*

EPHESIANS 5:18, 20

I have a beloved friend who has made it the habit of her life
to obey this injunction literally. When her husband's factory
was in flames, when her children were diagnosed with serious
illness, and when other apparent disasters befell her, she knelt
down to thank God. Why? Because she knew that He was a loving Father still, that He loved her too well to give her anything
but the best, and that He must love her very much to be willing to bless her at the cost of so much pain.

We may not always *feel* like thanking God for all things, but
let us always will and dare to do it. Let's not examine the crate,
but let's search within for the gift of love. Although at first sight
we may be disappointed and sad, whatever the Father sends
must be the very best. Dare to believe it, and you will come to
find it so. Thus we will learn to receive and know the Father's
peace and assurance. His peace will settle down on the troubled, restless heart as the evening, with its cool air and majestic
beauty, settles on the fevered landscape.

Reflection

Which challenging things in your life might God want you
to be thankful for? Why do you think God wants us to thank
Him for *all* things?

3

Use Your Mind Wisely

*"Then Paul, as his custom was, went in to them,
and for three Sabbaths reasoned with them
from the Scriptures."*

ACTS 17:2

God has given us wonderful faculties of brain power, and He earnestly desires for us to use them. In His grace, God does not cancel the action of any of His marvelous gifts, but He uses them for the communication of His purposes and thoughts.

It is greatly important, then, that we should feed our minds with facts, reliable information, results of human experience, and, above all, with the teachings of God's Word. It is a matter of the utmost admiration to notice how full the Bible is of biography and history, so that there is hardly a single crisis in our lives that may not be matched from those wondrous pages. There is no book like the Bible for casting a light on the dark landings of human life.

While the Scriptures provide our first and best source of guidance, there is no harm in taking pains to gather all reliable information that we may please God with our actions and decisions. It is for us ultimately to decide how God will teach us, but He may be speaking to us through the voice of sanctified common sense, acting on materials we have collected. Of course, at times God may bid us to act against our reason, but these are exceptional cases, and then our duty will be so clear that there will be no mistaking it. For the most part, God will speak in the results of deliberate consideration, weighing the pros and cons.

When Peter was imprisoned and could not possibly extricate himself, an angel was sent to do for him what he could not do for himself. But after they had passed through a street or two of the city, the angel left him to consider the matter for himself. Thus God treats us still. He will dictate a miraculous course by miraculous methods. But when the ordinary light of reason is adequate to the task, He will leave us to act and decide according to careful and logical thinking.

Reflection

What are some ways in which God has taught you? Why is it important for each of us to use our ability to reason in conjunction with the Bible?

Be Filled with God

*"Blessed are those who hunger and thirst
for righteousness, for they shall be filled."*

MATTHEW 5:6

In this life, as well as the next, it is possible to hunger no more and thirst no more. Not to hunger for the husks that the swine eat because we are filled with the provisions of the Father's table. Not to thirst for the pools at which the children of the world seek to quench their thirst because the pure water that springs up to eternal life is within. Not to clamor for crumbs and scraps that the world throws our way because there is so plentiful a provision of manna.

It is a blessed thing to be filled with the Spirit, to be full of joy and peace, to be fulfilled with God's grace and heavenly benediction, to be filled with the fruits of righteousness, to be filled with the knowledge of His will. The heart is restless until it is full, but when it has realized this blessed fullness, dipped deeply into the fullness of God and lifted out dripping with flashing drops, evil has no lure to charm, the fear of man cannot intrude, and the attractions of sin are neutralized. What more can the soul want than to be filled with You, O God, who made us for Yourself.

Reflection

Which people in your circles of influence do not yet know Jesus and are trying to quench their spiritual hunger and thirst with the wrong things? Pray that God will open up opportunities to share the fullness only God can provide.

7

Mind Your Motives

"The LORD searches all hearts and understands
all the intent of the thoughts."

1 CHRONICLES 28:9

We must be very careful in judging our motives, searching them as detectives search each person who enters a public building or event. When we have, by God's grace, been delivered from blatant forms of sin, we are still vulnerable to the subtle working of self during our holiest and loveliest hours. It poisons our motives. It breathes decay on our fruit-bearing. It whispers seductive flatteries into our ears. It turns the Spirit from its holy purpose, as the masses of iron on ocean steamers deflect the needle of the compass from the pole.

As long as there is some thought of personal advantage, some idea of acquiring the praise and commendation of men, some aim at self-aggrandizement, it will simply be impossible to find out God's purpose concerning us. The door must be resolutely shut against all these if we would hear the still, small voice. Ask the Holy Spirit to give you the good eye, and to inspire in your heart one aim alone: that which animated our Lord and enabled Him to declare, "I have glorified You on the earth" (John 17:4).

Reflection

Is your primary desire to glorify God? Ask Him to reveal to you any wrong motives in your life.

God Will Reveal His Plans

"*Stand still, and see the salvation of the LORD.*"

EXODUS 14:13

God's impressions within and His Word without are always corroborated by His providence around, and we should quietly wait until all three of these focus onto one point. Sometimes it looks as if we must act. Everyone says we should do something and, indeed, things seem to have reached so desperate a pitch that we must. Behind are the Egyptians; right and left are inaccessible precipices; up ahead is the sea. It is not easy during such times to stand still and see the salvation of God, but we must.

God may delay to come in the guise of His providence. There was delay before Jesus came walking on the sea in the early dawn or hurried to raise Lazarus. There was delay before the angel sped to Peter's side during the night before his expected martyrdom. God stays long enough to test patience of faith, but not a moment behind the extreme hour of need.

It's remarkable how God guides us by circumstances. One moment, the way may seem utterly blocked, then shortly afterward some trivial incident occurs that might not seem much to others but which to the keen eye of faith speaks volumes. Sometimes these signs are repeated in different ways in answer to prayer. They are not haphazard results of chance, but the opening up of circumstances in the direction in which we should walk. And they begin to multiply as we advance toward our goal, just as lights do as we near a populous town when riding through the land by night train.

After months of waiting and prayer, I have become absolutely sure of the guidance of my heavenly Father. With the emphasis of personal experience, I encourage each troubled and perplexed person to wait patiently for the Lord until He clearly indicates His will.

Reflection

How easy is it for you to wait for God's confirmation of His will? Are you confident that God will lead you in *His* timing?

Your Secure Position in Christ

"You are all one in Christ Jesus."
GALATIANS 3:28

Our experiences are as fickle as April weather—now warm, now cold; now sunshine, now cloud; now dry, now wet. But our standing in Jesus doesn't change. It is like Him—the same yesterday, today, and forever. Our sure position in Christ did not originate in us but in His everlasting love. It has not been purchased by us, but by His precious blood that pleads for us as mightily and successfully when we can hardly claim it as when our faith is most buoyant. It is not maintained by us, but by the Holy Spirit.

If we have fled to Jesus for salvation—sheltering under Him, relying on Him, and trusting Him—then we are one with Him forever. We were one with Him in the grave, one with Him on Easter morning, one with Him when He sat down at God's right hand. We are one with Him now as He stands in the light of His Father's smile. No doubt or depression can for a single moment affect or alter our acceptance with God through the blood of Jesus, which is an eternal fact.

Our standing in Jesus is our invested capital. Our emotions at best are but our spending money, which is always passing through our pocket or purse, never exactly the same. Cease to consider how you feel, and build on the immovable rock of what Jesus is, has done, is doing, and will do for you in times to come.

Reflection

When times are tough, how much do you trust in your feelings rather than remembering who you are in Jesus?

God Demands Obedience

*"If you are willing and obedient, you shall eat
the good of the land; but if you refuse and rebel,
you shall be devoured by the sword."*

ISAIAH 1:19–20

Sometimes a person comes to a spiritual advisor and says, "I have no joy, and I've experienced very little for years."

The older, wiser Christian asks, "Did you once have joy?"

"Yes, for some time after my conversion to God."

Again, the advisor asks a question: "Are you aware of a time when you refused to obey some distinct command, a directive from God that you ignored?"

Then the face is cast down, the eyes fill with tears, and the answer comes with difficulty: "Yes, years ago I used to think that God required a certain thing of me. I felt sure God was calling me to do something, but I did not heed the call. I did not do what He wished and was uneasy for some time about it. After a while, though, it seemed to fade from my mind, and now it does not often trouble me."

The mature Christian responds, "My friend, that is where you have gone wrong, and you will never regain your joy until you go back through the weary years to the point where you dropped the thread of obedience. Retrace your steps and complete that one thing God requested of you so long ago. Then watch and see how the burden is lifted."

Isn't this the cause of depression for thousands of Christian people? They are God's children, but they are disobedient to their Father. The Bible rings with one long demand for obedience. The key phrase of the book of Deuteronomy is this: "Observe and do." The cornerstone of Christ's farewell discourse is, "If you love Me, keep My commandments." We must not question, reply, or excuse ourselves. We must not pick and choose our way. We must not take some commands and reject others. We must not think that obedience in other areas will compensate for disobedience in another. God gives one command at a time, and He expects obedience. If we obey all along the way, He will flood our soul with blessing and lead us forward into new paths and pastures. But if we refuse to heed the Master's call, we will remain stagnant and waterlogged, lacking power and joy.

Reflection

In which areas of your life do you find it particularly difficult to obey God fully? Why do you think God calls us to *complete* obedience?

No "Small" Sins

*"Wash me thoroughly from my iniquity,
and cleanse me from my sin."*

PSALM 51:2

When water is left to stand, the particles of silt betray themselves as they fall one by one to the bottom. So if you are quiet, you may become aware of the presence in your soul of permitted evil. Dare to consider it. Do not avoid the sight as the bankrupt person avoids his telltale ledgers or the tuberculosis patient avoids the stethoscope. Quietly consider whatever wrongdoing the Spirit of God brings to light. It may have lurked in the cupboards and cloisters of your being for years, suspected but unjudged. But whatever it is, and whatever its history, be sure that it has brought the shadow over your life that causes unrest and turmoil.

Does your will refuse to relinquish a practice or habit that is contrary to the will of God? Is there some injustice you refuse to forgive, some bill you refuse to pay, some wrong you refuse to confess? Do you permit some secret sin to have its unhindered way in your life? God does not look upon our misdeeds as great or small, major or minor. Each transgression separates us from harmony with God's will for our lives.

Reflection

What came to mind as you read this? What may be keeping you from taking the action you know God wants you to take?

Live by Will, Not Just Emotion

"Now may the God of peace ... make you complete
in every good work to do His will, working in you
what is well pleasing in His sight."

HEBREWS 13:20–21

We have no direct control over our feelings, but we have control over our will. God does not hold us responsible for what we feel but for what we will. Furthermore, in His sight, we are not what we *feel* but what we *will*. Let us, therefore, not live in the summerhouse of emotion but in the central citadel of the will, wholly yielded and devoted to the will of God.

When we are in communion with the Lord, our soul is often flooded with holy emotion, the tides rise high, the swelling tides of joy rise, and every element in nature joins in the choral hymn of rapturous praise. But tomorrow comes, and life has to be faced in the trying workplace, the dingy shop, the noisy factory, the godless workroom. As the soul compares the joy of yesterday with the difficulty experienced in walking humbly with the Lord, it wonders whether it is quite as devoted and dedicated as it was. But during such a time, how reassuring it is to say with confidence that the *will* has not altered its position by a hair's breadth. We can sincerely declare, "My God, the spring tide of emotion has passed away like a summer brook, but in my heart of hearts, in my will, You know I am as devoted and as loyal to You as during the blessed

moment of communion with You." This is an offering with
which God is well pleased.

Reflection

Why is it important to live according to what we *will*, not
by what we *feel*? What makes this hard to do sometimes?

Focus on God's Heart, Not Your Own

"Delight yourself also in the LORD."

PSALM 37:4

The healthiest people do not think about their health, but the weak might induce disease by morbid introspection. That is, if you begin to count your heartbeats, you might disturb the rhythmic action of the heart. If you continually imagine a pain somewhere, you're likely to produce it. Likewise, there are some true children of God who induce their own darkness by morbid self-scrutiny. They are always going back on themselves, analyzing their motives, stewing over past transgressions, reliving regretful decisions.

To be sure, there are certainly times in our lives when we must look within and examine our heart. But this is only done that we may turn with fuller purpose to the Lord and His will for us. If we are forgiven by God, it is time to move on. We must not spend all our lives cleaning our windows or considering whether they are clean; instead, we should bask in the sunlight of God's joy streaming in through those windows. That light will soon show us what still needs to be cleansed away and will enable us to cleanse it with unerring accuracy. Dwell on your own heart only as much as is needed to find harmony with God's heart.

Reflection

What is the balance between taking responsibility for your actions and "letting go and moving on"? Do you think too much about yourself and not enough about God?

The Holy Spirit Reveals Deep Truths

"Attaining to all riches of the full assurance of understanding, to the knowledge of the mystery of God."

COLOSSIANS 2:2

There are deep things of God, mysteries, hidden things, of which the apostle Paul often speaks. The eyes of the natural man cannot discern, nor his ear detect, nor his heart conceive them. Higher than the vast heights above us or the fathomless lakes beneath, they defy the wise and prudent of this world. But they are revealed to babes—not in the land of light and glory, but here and now, through the grace of the Holy Spirit. God has revealed them to us by the Spirit (see Eph. 3:5). Jesus promised that when the Spirit of Truth came, He would lead us into all the truth and reveal the things of Christ to us.

Let us be apt pupils of so transcendent a teacher. Be willing and eager to receive what the Spirit reveals—and accept the mystery of that which He does not.

Reflection

What mysteries of the faith are particularly perplexing to you? What do you wish the Holy Spirit would reveal to you that He hasn't?

Walk Carefully, Abiding in God

"Walk in the Spirit, and you shall not fulfill the lust of the flesh."
GALATIANS 5:16

On life's path, be careful where you place your feet. Pick your way amid the pitfalls of the world. Gird up your robes with care, lest they be soiled by the filth of the street. Beware of any detours that would lead your steps away from the narrow track. Watch and pray. Especially be careful to turn every moment of time into an opportunity of making progress in the divine life. Take heed to the moments, and the hours will take heed to themselves.

All these injunctions, however, will baffle us and we will stumble along the way unless we blend with them the thought that God desires to walk with us—no, *in* us. He said, "I will dwell in them and walk among them" (2 Cor. 6:16). Abide in God, and God will abide in you, together every step and every mile of the journey.

Reflection

Looking back over your life, what "detours" have you taken? Reflect on how much God loves you and longs to draw you closer to Himself, to guide you in your walk with Him. Pray that He give you a heart that desires Him above everything else.

Love and Faith Are Inseparable

"I also, after I heard of your faith in the Lord Jesus and your love for all the saints, do not cease to give thanks for you."

EPHESIANS 1:15–16

When there is faith in the Lord Jesus, there will always be love toward all the saints because faith is the faculty of taking God into the heart. Faith is God-receptiveness. Faith appropriates the nature of God just as the expanded lung does the mountain air or as the child does the parent's gift. Faith, like a narrow channel, conveys God's ocean fullness into the lagoons of human needs.

Therefore, wherever faith links the believer to the Lord Jesus, His nature begins to flow into the waiting, expectant heart and then to flow out toward all the saints. The love of God knows no favorite sect. It singles out no special school. As the sun and wind of nature, it breathes and shines alike on all. It is cosmopolitan and universal. You cannot imprison it within the walls of any one Christian community. It laughs at your restrictions and with equal grace raises up witnesses and standard-bearers from all parts of the church. Thus as we become more like God, our love leaps all barriers to greet all saints and expends itself on the great world of men.

Reflection

What is God teaching you about faith and love? In what way(s) is your love from God reaching out to touch other people?

The Holy Spirit's Dwelling

"He will give you ... the Spirit of truth, whom the world cannot receive, because it neither sees Him nor knows Him; but you know Him, for He dwells with you and will be in you."

JOHN 14:16–17

We fail to recognize many things in ourselves and in nature around us that are true. But there is a reason many Christians remain ignorant of the presence of the Spirit who lives within: *He dwells so deep.* The Holy Spirit dwells below the life of the body, which is as the curtain of the tent. He dwells below thought and feeling, judgment and imagination, in the deepest reaches of the soul.

It is comparatively seldom that we go into the farthest reaches of our being. We are content to live the superficial life. We prefer to skim along the surface. We eat, drink, and sleep. We fulfill the desires of the flesh and of the mind. We make short incursions into the realm of morals, the sense of right and wrong that is part of the makeup of men. But we have too slight an acquaintance with the deeper and more mysterious chamber of the spirit. Now this is why the majority of believers are so unaware of the divine and wonderful resident dwelling within. Let us all look deep into our hearts and souls to see who has come to live there.

Reflection

What keeps people from delving into the Holy Spirit and His work in their lives? How in touch are you with the Holy Spirit?

Receive the Patience of Christ

*"Let patience have its perfect work, that you may be
perfect and complete, lacking nothing."*

JAMES 1:4

L ife is not easy for any of us. No branch escapes the pruning
knife, no jewel the wheel, no child the rod. People harass
and vex us almost beyond endurance. Circumstances strain us
until the cords of our hearts threaten to snap. Our nervous system is overtaxed by the rush and competition of our times. It is
an understatement to say we need patience.

We must pray for God's help never to indulge in unkind or
thoughtless criticism of others; never to utter the hasty word or
permit the sharp retort; never to complain except to God; and
never to permit hard and distrustful thoughts to lodge within
the soul. We must ask the Father to help us always be more
thoughtful of others than self; to detect the one bright spot in
the clouded sky; to be on guard when tempted toward bitterness and betrayal.

We cannot live such a life until we have learned to avail
ourselves of the riches of the indwelling Christ. Our heavenly
Father asks that we demonstrate patience and forbearance in
all things, and it is only through Him that we are able to do so.

Reflection

In which areas do you particularly need patience? Ask God
to help you develop endurance and long-suffering.

Christian Warriors Must Pursue Peace

"[You have] shod your feet with the preparation of the gospel of peace."

EPHESIANS 6:15

There is undoubtedly a reference in these words to Isaiah's vision of the messengers, who, with beautiful feet, speed across the mountains to proclaim the good tidings of the gospel. But there is the further thought that those who carry the gospel of peace must tread gently and softly.

If the gospel of peace is our message, the peace of God should adorn our face with a holy calm, breathe through our lips like a benediction, and diffuse itself like the dew of the Lord over the places of human rivalry and hatred. Ours should be the blessedness of the peacemakers. Our tread should be only in the paths of peace, except when the trumpet of God clearly calls us to war against the sins and injustices. As the apostle Paul admonished, "If it is possible, as much as depends on you, live peaceably with all men" (Rom. 12:18). So then, let us follow after things that promote harmony and thus lead by example for all who desire peace.

Reflection

Think about what it means to live in peace with everyone around you. In what ways might you, with God's help, improve in this area?

Receive Christ's Forgiveness

*"I write to you, little children, because your sins
are forgiven you for His name's sake."*

1 JOHN 2:12

In Jesus, every obstacle has been removed out of the way of your immediate forgiveness and acceptance. The dying Savior put away sin, bearing our offenses in His body on the tree, reconciling the world to Himself. You may not believe this, or feel the joy of it, but that does not alter the fact that it's true.

After the peace accord was signed between the North and the South in the Civil War, soldiers still hid in the woods, eating only berries and nearly starving to death. These same soldiers might have returned to their homes. They either did not know, or did not believe, the good news, so they went on starving long after their comrades had been welcomed by their wives and children. Theirs was the loss, but their failure in knowledge or belief did not alter the fact that peace was proclaimed and that the door was wide open for their return.

It is a fact that a person who trusts Christ is born into God's family and becomes a child. There is no doubt about this. You may not feel good, you may regret recent failure, you may be spending your days under a pall of dark depression. But if you have received Christ and truly trusted in Him, you have been born again. You may be a prodigal or inconsistent child, but you are a child of the loving, welcoming Father. Enjoy the fruits of your rightful relationship: Take the child's place at the Father's table and enjoy His smile.

Reflection

Is there something that hinders you from receiving God's forgiveness and welcoming embrace? Thank God for His willingness to forgive you and care for you as His child.

Base Your Faith on God's Faithfulness

"God is faithful, by whom you were called into the fellowship of His Son, Jesus Christ our Lord."

1 CORINTHIANS 1:9

We are saved and blessed by the faith that passes through the facts of our Savior's life to Himself. We rest not on the atonement, but on Him who made it; not on the death, but on Him who died; not on the resurrection, but on Him who rose from the dead; not in statements about Him, but in Him of whom they are made.

All faith that turns toward Jesus is the right faith. It may be as weak as the woman's touch on the hem of Jesus' garment. It may bring no trumpet's blast. It may be small and insignificant as a grain of mustard seed. It may be as despairing as Peter's cry, "Lord, save me!" (Matt. 14:30). But if its deepest yearning be, "Christ, help me," it is the tiny thread that will bring the lost soul through subterranean passages, in which it had been nearly overwhelmed, into the light of life.

True faith reckons on God's faith. He is absolutely faithful—faithful to His covenant engagements in Christ, faithful to His promises, and faithful to the person who at His clear call has stepped out into any enterprise for Him. We may lose heart and hope, our heads may turn dizzy and our hearts faint, lover and friend may stand at a distance, the mocking voices of our foes may suggest that God has forgotten or forsaken. But He remains faithful. He cannot disown the helpless child whom He has begotten because it ails. He cannot throw aside responsibilities He has assumed, He has made, and He must bear.

Often I have gone to God in dire need, aggravated by nervous depression and heartsickness, and said, "My faith is flickering out, and I am losing all hope. But You are faithful, and I am counting on You." Do not trouble about your faith; count on God's faithfulness. If He asks you to step out on the water, He knows that He can bring you safely back to the boat.

Reflection

How has God shown His faithfulness to you in the past? How might you exercise your faith in God's faithfulness today?

Serve the One True Master

*"No one can serve two masters; for either he will
hate the one and love the other, or else he will be loyal
to the one and despise the other. You cannot
serve God and mammon."*

MATTHEW 6:24

Our Lord uses two significant words—*mammon* (an old word for the god of wealth) and *serve*, the subjection of the slave to the whims of an owner. Our Lord puts in juxtaposition the two masters (God, the beneficent Father, and mammon, the god of wealth) and says everyone must choose between them. Whichever you elect to serve will become the supreme dominating force in your life, giving you no option, save the obedience of a slave.

Notice the peril of the Christian who is falling under the sway of covetousness, which the apostle Paul calls idolatry (see Col. 3:5 and Eph. 5:5). At the end of the process, be it longer or shorter, he will renounce entirely the service of God and become the slave of moneymaking. The slightest acquaintance with commercial circles gives evidence of the tyranny of mammon, which compels its slaves to toil day and night; demands the sacrifice of love and health, of home enjoyments and natural pleasure; insists that every interest shall be subordinate to its all-consuming service; and at the end of life casts its devoted, bankrupt, and penniless upon the shores of eternity. Let us not take this choice lightly, for we face it nearly every day. And the choice we make will have repercussions through eternity.

Reflection

Why can money so easily become an idol? Who or what are you serving?

Libels or Bibles?

*"Therefore humble yourselves ... casting all
your care upon Him, for He cares for you."*

1 PETER 5:6–7

God cannot be honored when a child of His bears a burden
with downcast and dejected countenance. As men of the
world look upon the faces of those who profess to be God's
children, and see them dark with the same shadows as are flung
across their own, they may well wonder what sort of a Father
He is. Whatever a man's professions, we cannot help but judge
him by the faces of his children. And if God is judged by the
unconscious report made of Him by some of His children, the
hardest things ever said against Him by His foes are not far off
the truth.

Under such circumstances, the unbeliever may fitly argue,
"Either there is no God, He is powerless to help, He does not
really love, or He is careless of the needs of His children. Of
what good will religion be to me?" We are either libels or Bibles;
warning signals or harbor lights; repellent or magnetic. Which
we are very much depends on how we treat our burdens.

The one cure for burden bearing is to cast all burdens on
the Lord. Whatever burden the Lord has given you, give it
back to Him. Treat the burden of care as you once treated the
burden of sin; kneel down and deliberately hand it over to
Jesus. Say to Him, "I entrust this to You. I cannot carry them,

but I commit them all to You to manage, adjust, and arrange. You have taken my sins; now take my sorrows." As we find peace amidst hardship, others will know that God is faithful and trustworthy.

Reflection

What burdens do you need to hand over to God? How can you better give hope to others in the midst of adversity?

Holy Living: Our Greatest Work for God

"We are ambassadors for Christ."

2 CORINTHIANS 5:20

*B*eing is *doing*. Our greatest work for God and man is to *be*. The influence of a holy life is our greatest contribution to the salvation and blessing of the world. Although you cannot preach, teach, or engage in some sphere of Christian service, do not be greatly moved if "only" you can live the life of God among men. For thirty years, our Lord was content to live an absolutely holy life, as the Lamb of God without blemish and without spot. His supreme work in the world was not only to give His life as a ransom, but to live His life that He might leave us an example, that we should follow in His steps.

Too many Christians seem to think that the main object of life is to engage in a sphere of direct service, while they leave their personal character to take care of itself and to develop almost haphazardly. In truth, our main thought and care should be that Christ be formed in us and revealed in every look and gesture, word and act. Out of that will come naturally, inevitably, and blessedly our direct Christian service. The best work is that which arises out of the simplicity and beauty of our witness for truth and love.

Reflection

Why do so many Christians overlook personal character issues? Ask God to reveal to you any areas of thought and action that are hindering your service for Him.

25

Discovering True Strength

*"Some trust in chariots, and some in horses; but we will
remember the name of the LORD our God."*

PSALM 20:7

There is no limit to the spiritual power we may receive and
exercise. It is said of the Gadites who came to David,
while he was in the stronghold, that the least was equal to a
hundred and the greatest to more than a thousand (see 1
Chron. 12:14). And this might be typically true of each of us.
We might, like Micah, be "full of power by the Spirit of the
LORD, and of justice and might" (Mic. 3:8).

There is one preliminary condition, however, that we must
fulfill. We must be weak enough—willing to renounce the use
of those sources of success on which others boast. We must be
content that the thorn in the flesh, or the test of the stream, or
the wrestle at the ford of Jabbok should reveal our utter helplessness. In short, we must know and make known that we rely
upon the power of Christ. When we are weak, we will be
strong.

Reflection

Why is it so contrary to our nature (and especially in this
day and age) to admit our weakness and reliance on someone
other than ourselves? Why does God want you to trust fully in
Him and not in anything or anyone else?

Promote Peaceful Living

"Let the peace of God rule in your hearts."

COLOSSIANS 3:15

God is the center of peace, and from Him ever-widening circles of peace are spreading through the world. Let Jesus Christ utter His words, "Peace to you" (Luke 24:36) and breathe upon you the spirit of tranquility and say, "Receive the Holy Spirit" (John 20:22). Let that peace stand guard at your heart's gate.

Promote peace with all men. Always carry serene calm in your heart and the placid look on your face. Let there be no jarring, irritated note in your voice. Let all your movements be consistent with the rhythm of God's perfect peace. And then at night, having done all—by your demeanor, words, and behavior—to instill peace into this troubled world, return to your Father's arms, as a little child who has been at school all day amid rough companions, but joyfully arrives home at night. Steep your weary soul in His infinite restfulness and tell Him all your anxiety concerning yourself and others. Find shelter in God's protective presence, which will enable you to go forth again tomorrow on a similar mission. In this way, you will shed the peace of heaven over the sorrows and troubles of Earth.

Reflection

Which anxieties trouble you today? Share them with Jesus. Allow His peace to fill and equip you to bring peace to others.

God Faithfully Carries Our Burdens

"Whenever I am afraid, I will trust in You."

PSALM 56:3

Will not our Lord Jesus be at least as true and faithful as the best earthly friend we have ever known? Each of us has times when we are too weary or troubled to help ourselves—and thankfully, we can hand over our anxiety to our strong, trustworthy friend, who will gladly bear our burden.

Of course, there are a few *conditions* we must fulfill before we can leave our troubles with Jesus in perfect confidence. We must have cast our sins on Him before we can cast our cares. We must be at peace *with* God before we can have the peace *of* God through His gracious intervention on our behalf. We must also be living according to God's plan, obeying His laws, and executing His plans so far as we know them. We must also feed our faith with God's promises because this food is essential to make it thrive. With these things tended to, we may with perfect confidence trust in Jesus to lighten our load and carry our concerns.

Reflection

Which small or large cares might you give to God today? Are you meeting the conditions the author mentioned here?

Cultivate Openness with God

"Wait on the Lord, and keep His way."

PSALM 37:34

Since I have been forbidden by doctors to use my eyes for reading while riding on a train, I have learned some wonderful lessons. Sitting quietly in the carriage, I have sought to unite myself with God, not asking Him to help me, but asking if I may help Him. I seek not His sanction on my plans and designs but seek permission to participate in His plans and designs. It has been a fruitful experience; I see how it is possible to cultivate God's presence and endeavor to know His heart.

We must cultivate this openness of heart toward God. There must be no lie in our life, no lack of transparency, no concealment or withholding. All the secrets of heart and life must be laid bare before Him. We must avoid any attempt to seem more or better than we are. And before we give or pray or fast, we must quietly reveal the soul to God, silence every voice, screen all disruptions. Thus God's smile will become the supreme object of our endeavor, as we admonish ourselves, saying, "My soul, wait only upon God, for my expectation is from Him."

Reflection

Are you trying to keep any part of your life secret because it is sinful? Is your heart open before Him? Think about the attitudes of your heart and mind, and ask God to cultivate within you a deeper sense of His presence.

God Walks with You through Adversity

"Surely He has borne our griefs and carried our sorrows."
ISAIAH 53:4

You are passing through a time of deep sorrow. The love on which you were trusting has suddenly failed you and dried up like a brook in the desert—now a dwindling stream, then shallow pools, and at last drought. Perhaps the savings of your life have suddenly disappeared. Instead of helping others, you must be helped. Maybe your employment, and with it your income, has been abruptly taken away. It could be that your health is failing, and the anguish of anticipating the future is almost unbearable. In other cases, there could be the sorrow of loss through a severed relationship or even death.

During such times, life seems almost unsupportable. Will every day be as long as this? Will the slow-moving hours ever again quicken their pace? Will life ever regain its joy and lightness? Has God forgotten you in your moment of need?

Jesus Christ trod this difficult path, leaving traces of His blood on its stepping-stones. Apostles, prophets, confessors, and martyrs have passed by the same way. It is comforting to know that others have traversed the same dark valley and that the great multitudes that stand before the Lamb, wearing palms of victory, came out of great tribulation. Where they were, you may be now; and, by God's grace, where they are, you will be.

Reflection

Do you sometimes feel alone in the midst of hardship? Ask God to reveal Himself to you and assure you that you are not on your own during times of sorrow.

You Are Risen with Christ

"If then you were raised with Christ, seek those things which are above, where Christ is, sitting at the right hand of God."

COLOSSIANS 3:1

If!" someone will say. "Ah, there's the rub! I'm afraid that is not true of me. My life is sinful and sorrowful. There are no Easter chimes in my soul, no glad fellowship with the risen Lord, no victory over dark and hostile powers." But if you are Christ's disciple, you may affirm that you are indeed risen in Him. With Christ you were placed in the grave, and with Him you have been resurrected and triumphed over sin and death. The whole church—all who believe in our Lord Jesus—has passed into the light of the Easter dawn.

It is up to us to begin from this moment to act as if it were a conscious experience, and as we dare to do so, we will have the experience. Realize that Christ is your life—He is alive in you! See to it that nothing hinders the output of His glorious indwelling. Then live with the full knowledge that you share in Christ's victory.

Reflection

Even if we don't feel as if we have been raised with Christ, why is it important for us to consciously live in the certainty that we have? What does it mean to "seek those things which are above"?

Battle Evil with God's Power

*"We do not wrestle against flesh and blood,
but against principalities, against powers, against the rulers
of the darkness of this age, against spiritual hosts
of wickedness in the heavenly places."*

EPHESIANS 6:12

We are seated with Christ above the power of the enemy, but we are still assailed by it in our daily experience. The darkness of the world is the veil beneath which malignant and mighty spirits set themselves against the Lord. What are we that we may hope to prevail, either in our own temptations or in our efforts to dislodge them from human wills, unless we have learned to be empowered in the Lord and in the strength of His might?

Jesus has become, through the mighty act of His ascension, the storehouse of spiritual force, which has proved itself to be more than a match for all the power and craftiness of Satan. Jesus holds in Himself an abundance of spiritual power, a power that will ultimately result in the binding of Satan and the destruction of his realm. That power has not yet been fully exerted, but it is nevertheless in Him and available to us. We may "be strengthened with might through His Spirit in the inner man," and may "be strong in the Lord and in the power of His might" (Eph. 3:16; 6:10).

Reflection

Why do we each need the power of God in order to face Satan's power? What is involved in being empowered in the Lord, tapping into His "storehouse" of spiritual power?

Guard Your Mind

"Set your mind on things above, not on things on the earth."
COLOSSIANS 3:2

The cross of Jesus stands between you and the constant appeal of the world, as when the neighbors of Christian in *Pilgrim's Progress* tried to induce him to return to the City of Destruction. This does not mean we are to be indifferent to all that is fair and lovely in the life God has given us; it means the cross is to separate us from all that is selfish, sensual, and seductive of the flesh, the lust of the eyes, and the pride of life (see 1 John 2:15–17).

The proverb tells us, "As he thinks in his heart, so is he" (23:7). With many of us, there is little attempt to guard our thoughts. The door of our heart stands open, with none to control the ingress or egress of the multitude of thoughts continually passing through. If only we would ask the Holy Spirit to control our thoughts, so that we might think only the things that are true and of good report, a wonderful change would come over our life.

Reflection

Why is it easy to rationalize our thoughts and not guard what we put into our minds? In what ways have your thoughts affected your life—for better or worse?

Discipline Yourself in Light of God's Truth

"Stand therefore, having girded your waist with truth."
EPHESIANS 6:14

For Christians, there is a strong obligation to stand directly in front of the mirror of truth. This mirror reflects back the image of Christ—Christ, the light who illuminates the conscience, hidden deeds, and deepest thoughts of every person. There is no severer or straighter test than this. With unfailing accuracy, we will discover our true selves as we come face-to-face with Him.

If there is any obliqueness, irregularity, or inconsistency, it will be immediately revealed. No distortion of the inner life can escape detection or condemnation before the truth of Christ's inspection. Would that we were all in the habit of submitting to that faithful scrutiny, not the greater matters only but all the smallest details of our lives.

Let us, in the name and by the power of Jesus, put away all that has been shown to be inconsistent with His character and claims, and let us submit in everything to His control. It will cost us something. We may have difficulty with our judgment, warped and injured by self-preference. We may have to contend with our will, reluctant to sign the death warrant of some favorite habit. We may feel singularly powerless to carry into effect what we know, in our loftiest moments, to be our only safe and blessed policy. But happy are we, if we dare to catch up the trailing robes of self-indulgence and restrain them under the belt of inexorable truth and purity.

Reflection

How familiar are you with the truths of God revealed in the Bible? What does it mean exactly to hold your life up to the "mirror of Christ's truth"?

Jesus Walks with Us through Suffering

"Lo, I am with you always, even to the end of the age."
MATTHEW 28:20

Sorrow is a refiner's crucible. It may be caused by the neglect or cruelty of another, by circumstances over which the sufferer has no control, or as the direct result of some dark hour in the long past. But inasmuch as God has permitted it to happen, it must be accepted as His appointment and considered to be the furnace by which He is searching, testing, probing, and purifying the soul. Suffering searches us as fire does metals. We think we are fully for God until we are exposed to the cleansing fire of pain. Then we discover, as Job did, how much dross there is in us and how little real patience, resignation, and faith.

During sorrow the comforter is near, "a stronghold in the day of trouble" (Nah. 1:7). He sits by the crucible, as a refiner of silver, regulating the heat, noting every change, waiting patiently for the scum to float away, and His own face to be mirrored in clear, translucent metal. No earthly friend may tread the winepress with you, but the Savior is there, His garments stained with the blood of the grapes of your sorrow. Dare to repeat it often, though you do not feel it, and though Satan insists otherwise, "Jesus, you are with me." Say this again and again, and you will become conscious that He is indeed with you.

Reflection

Why is it sometimes difficult to believe Jesus is with us during times of trouble? How does suffering and sorrow refine our faith?

The Holy Spirit's Guidance and Comfort

*"But the Helper, the Holy Spirit ... will teach you
all things, and bring to your remembrance
all things that I said to you."*

JOHN 14:26

Understand that since you are Christ's, the blessed Comforter is yours also. He is within you as He was within your Lord. In proportion as you live in the Spirit, walk in the Spirit, and open your entire nature to Him, you will find yourself illuminated with the light of His glory. And as you realize that He is in you, you will realize that you are always in Him. Thus the beloved apostle wrote, "By this we know that we abide in Him, and He in us, because He has given us of His Spirit" (1 John 4:13).

Perhaps you say, "I know rationally that the Spirit is within me, but I so infrequently experience His power, guidance, and comfort. Why?"

It is because your life is so hurried. You do not take time enough for meditation and prayer. The Spirit of God cannot be discerned while the heart is occupied with anxieties, the pulse beats quickly, or the brain is filled with troubling thoughts. It is when water stands still that it becomes translucent and reveals the pebbly beach below. Be still, and know that God is within you and around you. In the hush of the soul, the unseen becomes visible and the eternal real. Let no day pass without silently waiting before God and allowing His Spirit to reveal Himself to you.

Reflection

What prevents you from spending more time in quietness and solitude so the Spirit might speak to you? How might you devote more time to listening to the Spirit's voice?

A Matter of Priorities

*"Beware of covetousness, for one's life
does not consist in the abundance
of the things he possesses."*

LUKE 12:15

en are often more eager to get God's help in temporary matters than in spiritual matters. The man in the crowd who appealed to Christ was more anxious that He should intervene on his behalf in a family dispute than to give him the life of the ages (see Luke 12:13). But our Lord refused to be judge and arbitrator. His ministry went deeper to the springs of action, and He knew that in each brother there was the root of covetousness, which led the one to wrong the other. He struck at the sin that lay at the root of all such disputes about property.

Our Lord insisted that life does not consist in the abundance of things we may happen to possess. We say, "That person is worth a million dollars!" Heaven estimates an individual's worth by the courage, faith, purity, self-control, and love toward God and man that have developed by the careful discipline of the years. Acceptance and rank in the kingdom of God depends on character, not possessions. How often man proposes and God disposes!

If you really wish to see life and know happy days, burn these words into your mind: "Seek the kingdom of God, and all these things shall be added to you.... For where your treasure is, there your heart will be also" (Luke 12:31, 34).

Reflection

What is most important to you? How is God's definition of what's important different from what many people today value?

Be Pure in Heart

"Blessed are the pure in heart, for they shall see God."
MATTHEW 5:8

To see the king's face was the ambition of loyal courtiers and subjects in the old days, when the Queen of Sheba congratulated Solomon's servants on being able to stand always before him. To Absalom, it was the keenest sign of disgrace that he was not allowed to see the face of the king, his father.

This is the thought that probably underlies the beatitude quoted above. Only the pure in heart can stand in the inner circle, searched by those eyes that are too pure to look on sin. Only unstained garments can pass muster in the throne room of the Supreme. This truth was symbolized in the purity of ablution that prevailed in the ancient tabernacle, and it remains true that no unclean man can see the Lord. If you and I would dwell in the secret place of the Most High, if we would dwell in the house of the Lord all the days of our life, we must be pure in heart.

Reflection

Are you pure in heart? Why or why not? If you stood before God right now, what might He say?

Imitate Christ's Sacrificial Love

"Walk in love, as Christ also has loved us and given Himself for us."
EPHESIANS 5:2

We are to imitate God's love in Christ. It is the love that gives, that counts no cost too great and, in sacrificing itself for others, offers all to God and does all for His sake. Such was the love of Jesus—sweet to God, as the scent of fields of newly mown grass in June. This must be our model. We ought to love not only those who are agreeable, but also those who offend; not only those who love us, but also those who hate. Every time we sacrifice ourselves for the sake of the love of Christ, we enter into the meaning of the sacrifice of Calvary, and a sweet fragrance is wafted up to God.

Reflection

Is there someone you have a hard time loving? How would you respond to this person if you were to imitate God's love in Christ?

Claim Your Promised Portion

"Be filled with the Spirit."
EPHESIANS 5:18

Charles Spurgeon said once that he never passed a single quarter of an hour in his waking moments without a distinct consciousness of the Lord's presence. When the Spirit fills the heart, Jesus is vividly real and evidently near. What is He to you? Do you awake in the morning beneath His light touch and spend the hours with Him? Can you frequently look up from your work and perceive His face? Are you constantly seeking from Him power, grace, direction?

The injunction to "be filled with the Spirit" is as wide-reaching in its demands as "husbands, love your wives" (Eph. 5:25), which is found on the same page. It is a positive command, which we obey to our benefit. All God's commands are enabling and empowering. In other words, He is prepared to make us what He tells us to become. On the day of Pentecost, in words that are the charter of our right to the fullness of the Holy Spirit, the apostle Peter told the listening crowds that the fullness that had suddenly come on them from the ascended Lord was not for them only or for their children, but for as many as were afar off, even for them whom the Lord God will call.

Are you one of His called ones? Then rejoice because that fullness is for you! Lay claim to the promised portion, and thank God for having cast your lot in an age of such marvelous possibilities.

Reflection

What does it mean to be *filled* with the Spirit? How can we experience the fullness of the Holy Spirit in our lives?

40

Don't Neglect the Bible's Guidance

"How sweet are Your words to my taste, sweeter than honey to my mouth! Through Your precepts I get understanding; therefore I hate every false way."

PSALM 119:103–104

Some earnest people have magnified the inner light and leading of the Holy Spirit to the neglect of the Word that He gave, and through which He still works on human hearts. This is a great mistake and the cause of all kinds of evil. As soon as we put aside the Word of God, we lay ourselves open to the solicitation of the many voices that speak within our hearts, and we have no test, no criterion of truth, no standard of appeal. How can we know the Spirit of God in some of the more intricate cases that are brought into the court of conscience unless our judgment is deeply imbued with the Word of God?

We must not be content with the Spirit without the Word, or with the Word without the Spirit. Our life must travel along these two, as the locomotive along the parallel rails. The Word is the chosen organ of the Spirit, and only by our devout contact with it will we be enabled to detect His voice.

We need a widespread revival of Bible study. The mines of Scripture, lying beneath the surface, invite discovery and drawing out. Those who obey the appeal and set themselves to diligent study will soon be aware that they have received the Spirit's filling.

Reflection

Why is Bible study so important in a Christian's life? What's the relationship between God's Word and the work of the Holy Spirit?

Use Your Influence Well and Wisely

"Let your light so shine before men, that they may see your good works and glorify your Father in heaven."

MATTHEW 5:16

What we *are* affects others much more profoundly than what we *say*. Waves of spiritual influence are continually going forth from our innermost nature, and it is the impact of these on those around us that makes it easier or harder for them to realize their highest ideals.

The first circle we can touch and influence is that of our friends. Our counsel may be sweetness or bitterness, but whatever we do or say, we must see that we are absolutely true and faithful (see Prov. 27:6, 9). Sincerity means to be without the wax that the cabinetmaker may put into the cracks of the wood to make it appear sound. It is the true and pure person who most readily and effectively helps another. Do not be selfish in your friendship, but always give out as *much* and *more* than you expect to receive.

The second circle of influence is that of our associates and acquaintances. The great world of men may not appreciate our reproduction of the Beatitudes of the kingdom, but may reproach, persecute, and say all manner of evil falsely. Nevertheless, we must continue to bless the world by the silent and gracious influence of holy living. It is wonderful how love and consistent, prayerful influence finally prevail. Inconsistency and cowardice are like bushels that are put over the lamp. Let us put away all these hindrances so that the light within us may shine out on the dark world.

Reflection

What kind of influence are you having on friends and acquaintances? What may be keeping you from being the light of the world God calls you to be?

42

Redeem the Time

*"Walk circumspectly ... redeeming the time,
because the days are evil."*

Ephesians 5:15–16

God desires to give each life its full development. Of course, there are exceptions. In some cases the lessons and discipline of life are crowded into a very brief space of time. But on the whole, each human life is intended to touch all the notes of life's organ. There is an appointed time when it will be born and die, weep and laugh, gain and lose, enjoy serene peace and endure storm-tossed seas. These times have been fixed for you in God's plan. Do not try to anticipate them or force the pace, but wait for the Lord's timing. In due course, all will work out for your good and for His glory.

Times and seasons succeed one another quickly. Indeed, as we look back on our life, it will seem as though each experience was only for a moment and then vanished, never to return. We must be on the alert to meet the demand of every hour. "My hour has not yet come," said our Lord (John 2:4). He waited patiently until He heard the hours strike in heaven, and then, drawing the strength appropriate to its demand, He went forth to meet it. The Father keeps each time and season in His own hand. And that same hand contains the needed supplies of wisdom, grace, and power. Take what is needed from His hand, and go forth to fulfill the duty for which the moment calls.

Reflection

How aware are you of what God might have you do today? Consider some ways in which you can better use your time and rely more on God's strength so that He is free to use you according to His timing.

43

Delight Yourself in the Lord

"Make a joyful shout to the LORD, all you lands!
Serve the LORD with gladness."

PSALM 100:1–2

The psalmist calls for a "joyful shout," an audible expression of worship. Do not be content with a quiet spirit of thankfulness—express it! It is good to let God have "the fruit of our lips." As a single bird can awaken a whole woodland choir, so a soul teeming with loving adoration will spread its own contagion of song. How often Christian people hinder the progress of Christianity by their dolefulness, depression, and downcast spirits. If we delight ourselves in the Lord, we should serve Him with gladness!

To be sure, there is much pain and sorrow in the world. We must dare to believe and affirm the goodness of God beneath all the distressing elements of modern life. With His goodness are combined His mercy and His truth. What comfort there is in knowing that His mercy is everlasting. We need so much patience, forbearance, and long-suffering, that if God's mercy were anything less we should despair, but it is extended to every generation until time shall be no more. Let us, therefore, demonstrate through word and deed all the hope and joy that is ours in Christ.

Reflection

Why do so many Christians fail to experience—or express—joy? What are some practical ways you might demonstrate more gladness and joy?

Quiet Time with God

"Be still, and know that I am God."
Psalm 46:10

The life around us is preeminently one of hurry and haste. Years are crowded into months and weeks into days. This feverish pace threatens the spiritual life. The rushing stream has already entered our churches and stirred their quiet pools. Meetings crowd on meetings. The same energetic people are found at them all and engaged in many good works besides.

We must make time to be alone with God. The closet and the shut door are indispensable. We must escape the din of the world to become accustomed to the accents of the still, small voice. Like David, we must sit before the Lord. Sit, wait, listen, be still. Only during such moments will the best spiritual gifts loom on our vision and we will have grace to receive them. It is impossible to rush into God's presence, catch up anything we fancy, and run off with it. To attempt this will end in mere delusion and disappointment. God's best cannot be ours apart from patient waiting in His holy presence.

Reflection

How much do you value quiet moments with God? Why are such moments vital to your spiritual growth?

Examine Your Motives

"Christ will be magnified in my body, whether by life or by death."
PHILIPPIANS 1:20

I f you want the fullness of the Holy Spirit so you may realize a certain experience, attract people to yourself, or transform some difficulty into a stepping-stone, you are likely to miss it. You must be set on the one purpose of magnifying the Lord Jesus in your body, whether by life or death. Ask that all inferior motives may be destroyed and that this may burn strong and clear within you.

God will not find water for us to use for turning our own waterwheels. He will do nothing to minister to our pride. He will not give us the Holy Spirit so we might gain celebrity, procure a name, or live an easy, self-contented life. If we seek the Spirit merely for our happiness, comfort, or liberty of soul, it will be exceedingly unlikely that He will be given. His one passion is *the glory of the Lord Jesus*, and He can only make His abode with those who are willing to be at one with Him in this.

But if you are motivated simply by the desire that the Lord Jesus may be magnified in you, whether by life or death, then rejoice, because you are near blessing beyond words to describe. If your motives fall below this standard, trust in Him to enlighten and purify them, and offer Him a free entrance within. It will not then be long before there will be a gracious response.

Reflection

In what ways are you magnifying the Lord in what you say, do, and think? Which motives do you need to ask Him to change?

Work as unto God

"[Serve] as to the Lord, and not to men."
EPHESIANS 6:7

The common drudgery of daily life can be a divine calling. We often speak of a young man as "being called to the ministry," but it is as fitting to speak of a carpenter being called to the workbench, the blacksmith to the forge, and the shoemaker to his wooden or metal form of a foot. "Brethren," said the apostle, "let each one remain with God in that calling in which he was called" (1 Cor. 7:24).

Remember that your life has been appointed by God's wise providence. God as much sent Joseph to the drudgery and discipline of the prison as to the glory and responsibility of the palace. Nothing happens to us that is not included in His plan for us, and incidents that seem most tiresome are often designed to give us opportunities to become nobler, stronger characters.

We are called to be faithful in performing our assigned duties. Not brilliance, not success, not notoriety, but the regular, quiet, and careful performance of trivial and common duties. Faithfulness in that which is least is as great an attainment in God's sight as in the greatest.

Take up your work, then, you who seem to be the nobodies, those tireless and faithful servants who draw little attention. Do it with a brave heart, looking up to Him who for many years toiled at the carpenter's bench. Do everything as in His presence and to win His approval. Look for opportunities to cheer your fellow workers. Do not complain or grumble, but let your heart rise from your toil to God—your maker, Savior, and friend.

Reflection

Why is it important to trust in God's plan for you and faithfully perform common duties for Him? What duties has God given you to fulfill?

Support the Cause of Christ Financially

"Bring all the tithes into the storehouse, that there may be food in My house."

MALACHI 3:10

If you are in business, at the end of the year put aside what is needed for the maintenance of your family in the position to which God has called them. Next, put aside what may be required for the development of your business. Third, be sure that by a system of life insurance you are providing for the failure of old age. But when all this is done, look on the remainder as God's, to be used for Him. Never give God less than a tenth, but give Him as much more as possible. If you have money by inheritance, you have no right to give that away or squander it; pass it along just as you received it, acknowledging that it is God's, awaiting your administration as His steward and trustee.

Let every Christian adopt the principle of giving a certain proportion of the income to the cause of Christ. Whenever the fascination of money begins to assert itself, instantly make a handsome donation to some needy cause. Every time the temptation comes to look at money from a selfish standpoint, meet it by looking up to God and saying, "Thank You for giving me these things to enjoy, and I desire wisdom and grace to use them for Your glory."

Reflection

Do you think you use your money wisely for the cause of Christ? How would you characterize your attitude toward money?

Take Every Sin Seriously

"Pursue ... holiness, without which no one will see the Lord."
HEBREWS 12:14

Every permitted sin encrusts the windows of the soul with thicker layers of grime, obscuring the vision of God. But every victory over impurity and selfishness clears the spiritual vision. In the Holy Spirit's power, deny self, give no quarter to sin, resist the Devil, and you will see God. The unholy soul could not see God even though it were set down in the midst of heaven.

The perpetual filling of the Holy Spirit is only possible to those who obey Him *in all things.* There is nothing trivial in this life. By the neglect of slight commands, a person may speedily get out of the sunlit circle and lose the gracious plentitude of Spirit-power. A look, a word, a refusal may suffice to grieve Him in ourselves and to quench Him in others. Count the cost, yet do not shrink back afraid of what He may demand. He is the Spirit of love. He loves us too well to cause grief, unless there is a reason, which we should approve if we knew as much as He.

Reflection

What happens when we allow "small" sins to remain in our lives? Ask God to reveal any such sins ... and confess them to Him.

The Unity of the Bible

"All Scripture is given by inspiration of God."
2 TIMOTHY 3:16

The world is full of religious books, but the man who has fed his spiritual life upon the Bible will tell in a moment the difference between them and the authoritative, inspired Scriptures. The eye can instantly detect the absence of life in the artificial flower; the tongue can immediately and certainly detect the absence or presence of a certain flavor submitted to the taste; and the heart of man, his moral sense, is quick to detect the absence in all other religious books of a certain savor that pervades the Bible.

In the possession of this mysterious attribute, the Old and New Testaments are one. You cannot say there is more of it in the glowing paragraphs of the apostle Paul than in the splendid prophecies and appeals of the ancient prophets. From Genesis to Revelation, there is wisdom, truth, and guidance. Throughout, there is silence on topics that merely gratify curiosity, but on which other professed revelations have been copiously full. Throughout, the crimson cord of sacrifice is clearly manifest, on which the books are strung together as beads upon a thread. And throughout, there is always the subtle, mysterious, ineffable quality called *inspiration*. Scripture is the speech of God to man. This gives it unity and authority.

Reflection

Are you studying the Bible, discovering how the Old and New Testaments relate to one another and to your life today? What does it mean that God's Word has "unity and authority"?

Angels among Us

*"Are they not all ministering spirits sent forth to minister
for those who will inherit salvation?"*

HEBREWS 1:14

From every part of Scripture come testimonies to the existence of angels. They rejoiced when the world was made, and they are depicted as ushering in with songs the new creation for which we long. They stood as sentries at the gate of a lost paradise, and at each of the twelve gates of the New Jerusalem an angel stands (see Rev. 21:12). They trod the plains of Mamre and sang over the fields of Bethlehem. One prepared the meal on the desert sands for Elijah, another led Peter out of jail, and a third flashed through the storm to stand by the hammock where the apostle Paul was sleeping (see Acts 27:23–24).

When we struggle against overwhelming difficulties and face danger of all kinds, we are surrounded by invisible forms, like those that accompanied the path of Jesus, ministering to Him in the desert, strengthening Him in the garden, hovering around His cross, watching His grave, and accompanying Him to His home. They keep pace with the swiftest trains in which we travel. They come unsoiled through the murkiest air. They smooth away the heaviest difficulties. They bear us up in their hands, lest we should strike our foot against a stone. Many an escape from imminent peril, many an unexpected assistance, many a bright and holy thought whispered in the ear is due to those bright and loving spirits.

Reflection

How do you think angels specifically function in the life of believers? Have you ever sensed the protection of angels in your life? What were the circumstances?

Christ, Our Friend

—◦◦◦—

"I have called you friends, for all things that I
heard from My Father I have made known to you."

JOHN 15:15

I read somewhere that when Michelangelo was in the height of his fame, a boy named Raphael—destined to be his worthy successor—was introduced to him as a promising pupil. At first the lad was employed in the simplest duties of the studio, cleaning brushes and mixing paints. But as he developed the qualities of exactness, punctuality, and sympathy, he became entrusted with increasing responsibility until the master made him his friend and confidant. So we come to Christ: first as redeemed from Satan's slavery, to be His servants; and then He calls us His friends.

A friend will reveal himself. All the world may suppose that it knows a famous man, but if *he* calls me his friend, I expect to get closer to him and hear from his lips items of confidential information. Thus it is with the Lord Jesus. He manifests Himself to those who love Him and keep His Word, as He does not to the world.

A friend will interest his friends in his undertakings. It is a joy to Christ when those whom He loves are able to share in His worldwide redemptive plans. Jesus is glad to have us as His fellow workers.

A friend will be interested in our failures and successes. It's the same with our Lord. When He sees some peril menacing us, does He not make the trial-hour one of special intercession? If we fail, He meets us intensely sorry, ready to point out the cause of our failure and encourage us to try again. If we stand our ground, He meets us as we come forth from the fight, glad for us, eager to refresh us in our weariness, careful to heal any wound we may have received.

Reflection

How do you view Jesus? How committed are you to obeying Him and participating in His plans?

Pursue the Guidance of God

*"I am the light of the world. He who follows
Me shall not walk in darkness, but have the light of life."*

JOHN 8:12

The wilderness was a trackless wasteland to Israel. The people absolutely depended on the cloud to reveal their path and find a resting place at night. When the cloud gathered itself up from the tabernacle on which it brooded, the people were to strike their tents and follow. However desirable their campsite was, they had to leave it. However difficult the desert paths, they had to traverse them. However uninviting the spot where the cloud stopped, they had to halt there and remain as long as it tarried. Only where the cloud rested did manna fall, water flow, or divine protection avail.

There are resting times in our lives. God graciously arranges green pastures and quiet waters, and makes us lie down. His voice sounds amid the turmoil of our existence and invites us to come aside and rest awhile. But often we fret against enforced rest; we persist in hurrying to and fro, and give way to bitter complaining. When the cloud stays, remain where you are. When you don't know what to do, stop still until some indication reveals your path.

There are also times for action. The trumpet is heard with its summons, to which we must give immediate attention. We will gain keenness of hearing when we accustom ourselves to instant obedience. The peace and usefulness of our earthly life will be in direct proportion to our appropriation of the Lord Jesus for all the demands of our pilgrim condition.

Reflection

Looking back over your life so far, when has God guided you? Why is it so hard to wait for God's guidance sometimes?

Trust God Completely

"Blessed is that man who makes the LORD his trust."

PSALM 40:4

It is better to trust in God than to accumulate riches. The moth and rust destroy, thieves steal, all earthly things are perishable and precarious. How many people have placed their savings in stocks and shares, in banks and companies, and have lost every penny. Others who have been unable to save and have lived to help their fellow men have found that God has made provision for them.

Trust in God gives clearness of vision. When we are thinking partly of doing God's work in the world, and partly of lining our own nest, we are in the condition of the man whose eyes don't look in the same direction. There is a squint in our inner vision. We are endeavoring to serve two masters, and our judgment is therefore distorted. Who has not often experienced this? You have tried to ascertain God's will, or form a right judgment about your life, but constantly your perception of duty has been obscured by the thought that, if you decided in a certain direction, you would interfere with your interests in another. Your eye has not been single, and you have walked in darkness. When, however, you feel so absorbed in God's interests that you are indifferent to your own, all becomes clear, and you leave Him to care for all results.

Let's not think that God is miserly and stinting in His gifts. He gives fish as well as bread when He feeds the crowds, colors as well as leaves when He clothes the flowers. You have been adopted into His family and may call Him "Abba, Father." Surely this act of grace shows a special love on His part. Would He have taken such care of the spiritual and have none for the physical? The ungodly may worry about their maintenance, but a child of God may be sure that his needs will be supplied.

Reflection

In whom or in what do you *really* trust? Why, in our culture today, is it so easy to have divided focus?

Share Christ's Love

"I am the vine, you are the branches."
JOHN 15:5

The vine itself cannot bear fruit of its own accord. It is only the channel along which the energy of God flows in its endeavor to gladden the heart and life of man. So Jesus is the channel through which the life and love of God reach us, that we may pass them on in loving ministry, and in so doing we create and store up for ourselves infinite joy.

Let each of us learn to abide in Christ. With the heart open to Him on the one hand, and open to men, women, and children on the other. Then let us trust Christ to pour His love and grace into our hearts, that the pressure within may lead us to perform acts of tender sympathy and helpfulness of which we would not otherwise have been capable. Let us resolve to let no day pass without doing something at cost to ourselves, to make the burden lighter and the path easier for someone else. Our willingness for Christ to do these things through us will always meet a response from Him; and His Spirit in us will show us exactly what to say or do. It may be only a smile, a touch of the hand, or a word. Thus life will be filled with joy.

Reflection

What is the connection between receiving God's love and being able to share it with others? Ask God to guide you to someone this week who needs what Christ can offer through you.

The Amazing Grace of God

*"God is able to make all grace abound toward you,
that you, always having all sufficiency in all things,
may have an abundance for every good work."*

2 CORINTHIANS 9:8

What shall we say of God's grace? His joy is unspeakable, His peace passes understanding, His love is beyond knowledge! Get great thoughts of God, who holds the ocean depths as a drop in the hollow of His hand. Lie on a bank of flowers and consider their multitude. Sweep the skies with a telescope and try to count the stars. Number the sand grains on the shore and count the shells strewn along the strand.

When you have considered the gifts of God's hand, ascend to the wealth of His heart. Study the infinite map of God's nature. Compare it with the need of your little life and then remember that the Father loves you infinitely. He has set His love upon you and will certainly deliver you. He will set you on high because you have known His name. All the resources of eternity and infinity are at His disposal, and He can make all grace abound toward you, that always having all sufficiency in all things you may abound to every good work.

Reflection

Why is it difficult to comprehend God's immense love for us? Think about God's deep love for you and why it is important for you to share what He gives you with other people.

Strength through God's Spirit

"Be strengthened with might through His Spirit in the inner man."
EPHESIANS 3:16

Who among us does not long for strength, whether to endure suffering or to accomplish greater feats? The sapling says, "Let me be strong, to bear the harvest of the rich autumn fruit." The child says, "Let me be strong, that I may help mother carry her burdens and do her work." The ill person says, "Let me be strong, that I may resume my duties and again be productive."

The Christian says, "Let me be strong, that I may not faint or be weary, that I may with full vigor and vitality serve the Master." The strength of God awaits us, through His Spirit pouring into the inner man. Reader, I implore you, during moments of weakness and discouragement, to appropriate that strength in that measure. Remember, though, that it is only perfected in weakness and consummated in those who have no might.

Reflection

Where does our strength come from? How do we receive it when we are weak and discouraged? Why is God's strength perfected in our weakness?

The Source of True Maturity

<hr>

*"You will save the humble people, but
will bring down haughty looks."*

PSALM 18:27

At the beginning of the Christian life, we earnestly seek to acquire certain virtues and graces. We have read about them or seen them exemplified in others, until they have cast over us the spell of their fascination. We strive for them and sometimes congratulate ourselves on their partial attainment. *Surely*, the person says to himself as he compares the present with the past, *I am purer, humbler, gentler than I used to be!* There is an arraying in treasures and jewels, as when the young girl takes from her drawer one ornament after another that has been given by admirers and friends. Quite often this self-complacency is shattered by some terrible fall or by repeated failure until we come to see that we have no more claim to possess goodness than a room to possess light. These things are not our own, but received from Jesus and enjoyed only in proportion as we abide in Him and He in us.

I am not good, but Jesus is in me the source of goodness. I am not humble, but Jesus dwells within me, bringing every proud thought and imagination into captivity to Himself. I am not strong, but I receive Him who is made unto me wisdom, righteousness, sanctification, and redemption. In absolute dependence on the Savior, we exemplify that growing sense of need that is one of the sure signs of the humble and contrite heart that God will not despise.

Reflection

What does it mean to "absolutely depend" on Jesus? Why does this type of dependence lead to spiritual growth?

Forgiveness through the Blood of Christ

*"In Him we have redemption through His blood,
the forgiveness of sins, according to the riches of His grace."*

EPHESIANS 1:7

Our Father instantly and freely forgives us according to the riches of His grace. He yearns over the wayward and stubborn, who avert their faces from His. He grieves for their sins but grieves most of all that they do not seek forgiveness, along with the freedom, joy, and wholeness that comes with it.

When our hearts are contrite, humble, and open—when we sincerely repent all our wrongdoing—God forgives. And when He forgives, He does so not meagerly and reluctantly, but gracefully and abundantly. His forgiveness is worthy of Himself, apportioned to the wealth of His glorious being and according to the riches of His grace. He does more than forgive; He "will remember no more" (Heb. 8:12). Moreover, He takes the evil of sin and turns it into an opportunity for a deeper experience of His goodness. As Paul said, "Where sin abounded, grace abounded much more" (Rom. 5:20).

Reflection

Why is it so difficult for some Christians to accept the totality of God's forgiveness, that He "will remember no more"? Are you ever hesitant to seek God's forgiveness? If so, why?

God's Purpose for Your Life

~~~

"For this cause I was born, and for this cause I have come into the world, that I should bear witness to the truth."

JOHN 18:37

God created each of us with a purpose. He sent us forth to realize an ideal, to fulfill a purpose, to bear witness to some phase of truth. The potter takes in hand a lump of clay with a distinct design. He intends, when he places it on the wheel, to make of it a vessel to adorn a temple or palace, or he has in mind to serve some important use. The revolving wheel on the one hand, and his skillful craftsmanship on the other, will evolve and complete his purpose. Shall we, then, not ask ourselves whether we are fulfilling the divine purpose of what the apostle calls "the upward call" (Phil. 3:14)?

We may ask God, "Why did you make me like this? What is your purpose for my life?" But He doesn't always give an audible reply. His answer is often voiceless. It steals in upon the soul imperceptibly, and we *know* that we are fulfilling His purpose. If you are engaged in some difficult task that is evidently your duty, ask that the Savior and you be yoked together. If you are called to minister to people who seem unresponsive or unsympathetic, ask God that His will may be done through you. If in any circumstance you feel confused and aimless, ask the Father to align your will and desire with His own. He has a purpose for your life, and He does not want it to remain a mystery to you.

Reflection

Do you have a clear sense of God's purpose for your life? If not, how can you discover what He wants to accomplish through you?

Three Signs of Jesus' Inner Voice

"'Whatever He says to you, do it.' ... Jesus said to them, 'Fill the water-pots with water.' And they filled them up to the brim."

JOHN 2:5, 7

Don't forget the necessity of obeying the inner voice of Christ, which may be recognized by these three signs: It never asks questions but is decisive and imperative; it is not unreasonable or impossible; and it calls for an obedience that requires some sacrifice of our own way and will.

Not only should we respond to God's voice, but we should also do so with *full* effort and compliance. Our obedience should not be partway or halfhearted. It was a severe test of obedient faith for Jesus' listeners to fill up those big jars, which stood in the vestibule of the house. Each contained about twenty gallons, and as they were probably nearly empty, it was a long, tedious business to fill them, especially at a time when guests required other attention. And yet "they filled them up to the brim."

It may be a very small thing He asks you to do—to teach a class of children, visit some sick person, write a letter, speak a word of comfort, hold out the helping hand, give the glass of cold water—but see to it that your response is hearty and robust. An act that may seem insignificant or inconvenient may, in fact, become the greatest achievement of your life.

When the Lord calls you to copartnership, be sure not to say, "Please do not ask me!" No, serve Him to the brim. He never asks you to do one small act for Him without being prepared to add His almighty grace to your weakness. It is an amazing thing that He should want our help. Let us give Him a response that is overflowing with gratitude and eagerness.

Reflection

In which areas may God desire your obedience to His inner voice? What things may be holding you back from responding heartily to Him?

Jesus Knows Our Sorrows

*"In all their affliction He was afflicted, and the Angel
of His Presence saved them; in His love and in
His pity He redeemed them; and He bore them
and carried them all the days of old."*

ISAIAH 63:9

There is the affliction of ill health, which compels us to
stand aside and leave our tasks to others. The languor of
sleepless nights. The inactivity and loneliness of the long days.
The fear of being burdensome to others. The sense of helplessness and weakness. These are the ingredients of that cup that
many have to drink.

There is the affliction of poverty, when every door seems
closed against our appeal. There is the affliction of broken rela-
tionships. There is also the affliction of temptation. Jealousy,
pride, discontentment, self-will—these assail us from without,
and too often they find a response from within, as though there
were an accomplice in hiding.

Such are some of the problems and afflictions that darken
our experience. The mistake is that we face our troubles without God's fellowship consciously realized. We carry our
burdens, without casting them on the Lord and claiming the
grace that waits to help us in our hour of need. We do not realize that He has come down to deliver us because He knows our
sorrows.

Reflection

What afflictions are you or a loved one facing? To what extent have you turned to God for help? Why can we be sure that God understands our situation?

A Life Yielded to God Lives for Others

"I beseech you therefore, brethren, by the mercies of God, that you present your bodies a living sacrifice, holy, acceptable to God."

ROMANS 12:1

The first thing for all of us to do is to present ourselves to God as alive from the dead and our bodies as living sacrifices. The path of blessedness can be entered by no other gate. Only as we refuse to be conformed to this world, and yield ourselves to be transformed by the Holy Spirit, can we learn all that God will do for us. He is prepared to be and do all things in us, if only we will lie open to Him as the land lies open to the summer sun.

Those who live the yielded life do not need to ascertain God's will by signs. They recognize it by the whisper of His voice and the touch of His hand. As we refuse to be molded by the world, we give ourselves up to the transfiguring Spirit of God, that we might prove what is good, acceptable, and perfect. But more than that, we begin to live for others and draw by faith from the fullness of God, that we may minister to them correctly.

We can never realize divine ideals of service merely through reluctant, begrudging obedience. We must be compelled by a holy love for our Lord and one another. That holy love comes from Him.

Reflection

Are you yielding yourself fully to God, allowing Him to transform you? What steps can you take to participate in the special ministry God has in store for you if you love Him and seek to serve others?

Sometimes God Waits to Bless Us

*"Therefore the LORD will wait, that He may be gracious to you;
And therefore He will be exalted, that He may have mercy on you....
Blessed are all those who wait for Him."*

ISAIAH 30:18

Too often we have misinterpreted God's dealings with us. When He has tarried beyond the Jordan, in spite of our entreaties that He should hurry to save Lazarus, we have concluded that He was strangely neglectful. But, in fact, He was waiting, at no small cost to His heart, until we came to the end of ourselves and the way was clear for Him to work a more astounding miracle than we had dared to hope.

Our Lord waited until the Syrophenician woman fell helpless at His feet, with the cry, "Lord, help me!" that He might grant to her the favor she craved for her child. From His throne in heaven, He pursued the same method, waiting until the disciples in the upper room had reached the point of utter helplessness so He could pour out the Spirit at Pentecost. He waited until the little group of believers had exhausted every other measure, that He might release to them Peter from his prison. He waited until Paul had renounced self-sufficiency and confessed his weakness, that He might take him strong in His almighty power.

God's delays are not denials; they are not neglectful or

unkind. He is waiting with watchful eye and intent for the pre-
cise moment to strike, when He can give a blessing beyond our
expectation and hope.

Reflection

Why do you think God often waits to respond until we
reach the end of ourselves? Can you think of a time when you
thought God had neglected you, only to discover His intervention later on?

Seek God's Guidance

"When he brings out his own sheep, he goes before them;
and the sheep follow him, for they know his voice."

JOHN 10:4

Do you need guidance as to your path? Look to Jesus; it is always possible to discern His form, though partially veiled in mist. And when it is lost, be sure to stand still until He comes back to find and reestablish the blessed connection.

Sometimes He guides us to the rest of the green pastures and the quiet of the still waters. In other words, we are left through happy months and years to fulfill the ordinary, commonplace activities of life. At other times, we are guided from the lowland pastures up into the hills. The way is sunny, above us the precipitous cliffs, beneath the dark and turbid stream, but this is fine. We should not always be lying in the pastures or walking softly by the waters. It is good to climb the heights with their far view and bracing air.

In the late afternoon, the Shepherd may lead His flock back into the valleys, through the dark woods where the branches meet overhead and the wild beasts lurk in ambush. But we know that in one hand He has the rod or club with which to fight off anything that may attack, and in the other the crook to drag us out of the hole. Darkness, sorrow, or death do not prove that we have missed His guidance or taken the wrong path, but rather that He considers us able to bear the trial by faith in Himself.

Reflection

In which areas do you need guidance? Why is it so important to trust God's guidance even when your circumstances are uncertain or even dreadful?

Pray Confidently ... and Trust God

"When you pray, go into your room, and when you have shut your door, pray to your Father who is in the secret place."

MATTHEW 6:6

In prayer, there must be deliberateness—the secret place, the inner chamber, the fixed time, the shut door against distraction and intruders. In that secret place, the Father is waiting for us. He is as certainly there as He is in heaven. Be reverent, as Moses when he took the shoes off his feet. Be trustful, because you are having an audience with One who loves you more than any other. Be comforted, because there is no problem He cannot solve, no knot He cannot untangle.

God knows even better than we do what we need and should ask for. He listens to our pleas and requests, and He rejoices to meet our needs according to His holy plans. You may be sure that, in some way or other, your heavenly Father will meet your particular need. When you have definitely put a matter into God's hands, leave it there. Be assured that He has heard you and will respond.

Reflection

Do you ever doubt that God will answer your prayers? If so, how can you develop deeper faith in God's desire and ability to meet your need?

Joy in the Midst of Suffering

"Count it all joy when you fall into various trials, knowing that the testing of your faith produces patience."

JAMES 1:2–3

We are invited to count our trials as pure joy, since our patient endurance leads ultimately to the finished product of a holy character. All the trials and afflictions that beset us are seen and shared by our Heavenly Father. God did not save Israel from the ordeal of affliction, but passed through it with them (see Ex. 3:7–9; Isa. 63:9). Evidently there was a wise purpose to be served by those bitter Egyptian experiences. The same is true with us.

There is a reason for our trials that we don't understand now, but we will someday, when we stand in the light with God. Afflictions are not always punishment, although in some cases that may be so. More often we "have been grieved by various trials, that the genuineness of [our] faith, being much more precious than gold that perishes, may be found to praise, honor, and glory at the revelation of Jesus Christ" (1 Peter 1:6–7).

Let us therefore rejoice, and magnify His loving-kindness. What a theme is here for praise! Sweet psalms and hymns have floated down the ages, bearing comfort for countless people because those who wrote them passed through searching discipline. And it may be that we who have passed through great tribulation will be able to contribute notes in the heavenly music that the unfallen sons of light could never sing. The Psalter of Eternity could not be complete without the reminiscences, set to music, of the grace that ministered to us during our earthly trials and brought us up out of the furnace of pain.

Reflection

What types of difficulties have you faced? What are some things God has taught you through them—about Himself, about yourself, about other people? How have your difficulties affected your faith in God? Why?

Aim High

"I press toward the goal for the prize of the upward call of God in Christ Jesus."

PHILIPPIANS 3:14

The only hope of the young artist is that he should not be content with the standard that prevails in the provincial town of his birth, but aim after that presented in the greatest masterpieces. The only hope of the gosling born in the farmyard is that it should not be content to paddle in the pond that suffices for the ducks. The hope of the soul is to refuse comparison with those beneath and to keep the eye fixed on the righteousness of God as it is revealed in Jesus' life.

Let us apply the highest standards of righteousness and godly living to ourselves. Let us strive to fulfill our high calling so that we could be content to live alone with God, as the one all-satisfying food of the soul. Hudson Taylor said, "I have been forty years in China. I have *done* little there, but I have *learned* much, and this of all things: to live alone with God, to know God Himself, to know that His heart is love and that His heart actuates His hand to help." Here is an ideal after which we may well aspire.

Reflection

What is involved in keeping our eyes fixed on God's righteousness? What is the balance between accepting imperfection in ourselves and maintaining high standards?

The Importance of Holy Thinking

*"Whatever things are true, whatever things are noble,
whatever things are just, whatever things are pure,
whatever things are lovely, whatever things are of good
report, if there is any virtue and if there is anything
praiseworthy—meditate on these things."*

PHILIPPIANS 4:8

Purity of heart will ensure purity of life and conduct. This connection has been too often overlooked and the order forgotten. Many people have insisted on the careful regimen of the body, proper behavior, and worthwhile deeds. But the secret of purity lies deeper. Begin with the outward, and you may or may not affect the inward temper of the soul. Begin with the inward temper, and the effect on the outward will be immediate and transforming.

Purity of heart means *the control of the imagination*. Away from the realm of sense, there lies a world of illusion, the atmosphere of which is brilliant but deadly, enchanting but corrupting. Imagination can at will transport us there. Like a swift boat, it can convey us to those mystic shores. Disembarking, we can take our part in unseemly revels, while our face is buried in our hands in the attitude of prayer. No heart can be kept pure unless the imagination is kept sternly under control. It must not be permitted to bear us away into the world of unholy and sensuous dreams, or to introduce into the temple of the soul any picture that would taint or defile.

Reflection

How can Christians keep their imaginations under stern control when so much in our culture encourages us to do otherwise? How can you better guard your mind and imagination?

Our True Source of Power

"Now to Him who is able to do exceedingly abundantly above all that we ask or think, according to the power that works in us."

EPHESIANS 3:20

Man longs for power. The young man will give all he has for love; the older man counts no sacrifice too great for power. He who wields power is the idol of his fellows, even though it may be attained by trampling upon others. We are not wrong in longing for spiritual power, if only we desire it for the glory of our Master and the blessing of man.

Spiritual power is not a separate entity that we can possess independently of the Holy Spirit. The power of the spiritual world is the indwelling and inspiration of the Holy Spirit Himself. We cannot have it apart from Him. We are most evidently the subjects and vehicles of it when He resides within our yielded hearts. If we seek spiritual power, let us then make welcome its true source. Let us no longer speak of *it*, but of *Him*.

Reflection

How does this view of power differ from many people's view of power today? What does it mean to "make welcome" the source of true power?

Pursue the Mind of Christ

"Let this mind be in you which was also in Christ Jesus, who ... being found in appearance as a man, He humbled Himself."

PHILIPPIANS 2:5–6, 8

When our Lord stooped to live visibly among men, He refused to avail Himself of the homage due to His original nature. He had been in the form of God but was content to veil His glory, to assume the form of a servant, to be made in the likeness of men. He refused to use the attributes of His intrinsic deity so that He might manifest God's love, bear away the guilt of the world, and usher in eternal righteousness. Therefore He is exalted and bears evermore the name of Jesus—the Savior of the world.

The apostle says, "Let this same mind be in you." We must show a holy emulation—the willingness to stoop the lowest and follow the Master to the closest. The most urgent matter for each of us to consider is whether or not we have the mind which was in Christ, whether at any cost to ourselves we are manifesting God's love to those around us.

Reflection

What does it mean to "have the mind of Christ"? How can you better follow His example of humility and service?

Experiencing God's Salvation

"Take the helmet of salvation."

EPHESIANS 6:17

The Christian warrior must know God's salvation in his own experience. He must be saved from the guilt and penalty of sin before he can proclaim the abundance of God's forgiveness to the chief of sinners. He must know the gospel as the power of God unto salvation from the dominion of sin in his heart.

As the helmet glistens in the sunshine, so must the crown of the Christian's experience point upward to heaven and onward to the glory yet to be revealed. He must speak that which he knows and declare what he has seen and heard. When we are experiencing the power of God's salvation, we can declare it to others with a freedom and a power that needs no further corroboration. When men see the salvation of God exemplified in our own life and character, they will be prepared to accept it as indeed the Word of God.

Reflection

What happens if we share God's salvation with other people when it's not being demonstrated in our own lives? If we are not living life through the power of God, what are we communicating?

Our Sorrow: A Key to Blessing

"Blessed are those who mourn, for they shall be comforted."
MATTHEW 5:4

The conditions of human life that men naturally dread are shown by Jesus to be the elements out of which blessing becomes possible. Every sorrow carries in itself a clue to blessedness, and there is no sorrow for which there is not healing and help in Christ. In this soil grow all the herbs that are suitable for the healing of broken hearts. For all mourning, He has the oil of joy.

Let no mourner turn away from these words as though they were meant for everyone else. Do not assume this promise is only for those whose sorrow is great and extraordinary. Like all the blessings of the gospel, the words are for everyone. They can be safely and fully trusted. Whoever you are and whatever sorrow is gnawing at your heart, you will be comforted. The seed of a harvest of blessedness is hidden in these dark pods. An eternal weight of glory is within your reach that will make your present affliction, when reviewed from the distant future, seem light in comparison.

Reflection

In what ways can sorrow be turned into blessing? What has God taught you during times of mourning?

Understanding God's Deep Love

"Whoever is wise will observe these things,
and they will understand the lovingkindness of the Lord."

Psalm 107:43

There are many ways of understanding the loving-kindness and mercy of the Lord. We may know it as a matter of doctrine. The best way of increasing our knowledge of God's infinite nature is by the reverent study of His Word. What the bones are to the body, doctrine is to our moral and spiritual life. What law is to the material universe, doctrine is to the spiritual. The doctrines of grace are the jeweled foundations of a holy life.

We may also know God's loving-kindness by meditation. Would that we yielded more silent hearts to the Holy Spirit, that He might fix our vagrant thoughts on the love of Christ that passes knowledge. Regular times of reflection in God's presence will open our hearts more deeply to His love.

Then we may also know God's love sympathetically. Every time we sacrifice ourselves for others, or carry another's cross, in the glow of a warm heart we are feeling a tiny pulsation of His love.

Do we sufficiently praise God for His loving-kindness and compassion? We are keen to pray, to cry out for help, but do we stop to enumerate the mercies and render praise for them? Let us pause often to thank Him for His deep love for us.

Reflection

What other ways, besides those mentioned here, might help you understand God's love more deeply?

Watch Your Walk

"Walk worthy of the calling with which you were called."
EPHESIANS 4:1

As the shepherd calls to his sheep, as the parent calls to a child, so God calls people to Himself. From the throne of His glory, He speaks to every soul of man—once, twice, many times—as when He said, "Samuel, Samuel," and "Saul, Saul." During some solemn hour of decision or difficulty, God's voice may be heard calling men to Himself, to heaven, and to a saintly life. On that call, the apostle bases his argument for holiness.

Act worthily of the love that summoned you and the life to which you have been called. Stand still and ask yourself before you speak, act, or decide, *Is this worthy of that great ideal that God conceived for me when He called me from the rest of men to be His child, His witness?* If not, avoid it!

Reflection

How might your life be different if you asked yourself that question before you spoke, acted, or decided? To what kind of life is God calling *you?*

Delve Deeply into the Bible

*"When You said, 'Seek My face,' my heart said to You,
'Your face, LORD, I will seek.'"*

PSALM 27:8

There are many things in the Bible that, at first, we may not be able to understand. Why? Because as the heavens are higher than the earth, so are God's thoughts higher than ours. Charles Spurgeon used to say that when he ate fish, he did not attempt to swallow the bones but put them aside on his plate! He meant that when he came upon something in the Bible beyond his understanding, he put it aside and went on to enjoy morsels more easily digested.

God's Word does indeed contain many principles and concepts that are difficult to comprehend from our human perspective. There are times, as Mr. Spurgeon suggested, that we must set aside passages and return to them another day. But let us not shrink from *trying* to understand God's message to us and listening closely for His voice. Whether for the body, soul, or spirit, there is no guide like Holy Scripture, but never read it without first looking up to its author and inspirer, asking that He will illuminate the page and make you wise unto salvation.

Reflection

What is your response when you come upon a passage that's hard to understand? Why should we ask God to guide us in understanding and applying Scripture?

What It Means to Be Meek

"Blessed are the meek, for they shall inherit the earth."
MATTHEW 5:5

Meekness is consistent with strength of character, but is not always thought so. Meekness is often used as a synonym for weakness, and meek people are held in a considerable degree of contempt. There is no epithet that men of the world would more quickly and vehemently resent than the appellation "meek." A young officer would rather have a stone hurled at him than this. An absence of backbone and muscle are the ideas that generally come to mind when a person is called meek. How distorted is this characterization!

Man's misconception of the strength of meekness is largely due to the gentle guise it adopts—the restraint, the self-possession, the modulated tones. People do not realize that there is even greater force required to restrain the manifestations of power than in letting it loose. It is a stronger thing for a man of vehement and impetuous temper to act gently in the face of provocation than to blurt out indignant words and bluster like a northeast wind!

Is meekness equivalent to weakness? Certainly not. It is the meek whose quiet resolve and inconspicuous fortitude demonstrate true strength.

Reflection

Before you read this, what was your definition of meekness? Why is the truly meek person the strong one?

The Possibility of the Impossible

"The Lord said, 'If you have faith as a mustard seed,
you can say to this mulberry tree, "Be pulled up by the roots and
be planted in the sea," and it would obey you.'"

LUKE 17:6

All God's fullness will flow through the tiniest channel that faith opens to His almighty power. Faith is the open heart toward Him, and through the channel of faith Christ lives in and through us. Hudson Taylor heard God say, "I'm going to evangelize inland China, and if you will walk with Me, I will do it through you."

D. L. Moody said that the beginning of his marvelous ministry hinged on this remark made in his presence: "The world has yet to learn what God can do through a man wholly yielded to Him." What matters is not what *we do*, but what God does through us. His mighty power, passing through the tiniest aperture of faith, keeps hollowing it wider.

Reflection

Why does faith play such a key role in what God can do through us? How might you demonstrate faith in Him this coming week?

Called to Righteousness

*"Blessed are those who hunger and thirst for
righteousness, for they shall be filled."*

MATTHEW 5:6

The desire of the regenerate person is not simply toward God, but for righteousness. To be right, to do right, to conform in all things to God's ideal, to have a conscience void of offense, to live according to the example of Jesus—this is the desire of the regenerate person. It is not enough to be conscious of weakness and ignorance, or to mourn for sin. The true penitent desires to learn the secret of walking before God in holiness and righteousness all his days.

Our one regret should be that our desires after God and His righteousness are so fickle and faint. Holiness is a high calling, and we disregard it at our own peril. Let us take it to heart that we know so little of the passionate yearnings for God that have dwelt in all holy hearts. May God create in us hunger and thirst like that which Jesus knew, that we may be led by it to know the blessedness that comes from righteous living.

Reflection

What does it mean to "hunger and thirst" for righteousness? Why are so many people in our day nonchalant about pursuing righteousness?

The Refiner's Fire

*"You have been grieved by various trials,
that the genuineness of your faith, being much
more precious than gold that perishes, though it is
tested by fire, may be found to praise, honor,
and glory at the revelation of Jesus Christ."*

1 PETER 1:6–7

Nothing is harder to bear than the apparent aimlessness of suffering. They say that what breaks a convict's heart in prison is to force him to carry stones from one side of the prison to the other and then back again. But we must never view the trials of life as punishments, because all penalties were borne by our Lord Himself. They are intended to destroy the weeds and rubbish of our natures, as the bonfires do in the gardens. Christ regards us in the light of our eternal interests, of which He alone can judge. If you and I knew what sphere we were to fulfill in the other world, we would understand the significance of His dealings with us, as now we cannot do. The Refiner has a purpose for your troubles, though He alone knows what it is until the time of revealing.

Dare to believe that God is working out a plan in your life. He loves you! Speak to Christ in the midst of your daily toil. He hears the unspoken prayer and catches your whispers. Talk to Christ about your trials, sorrows, and anxieties. Make Him your confidant in your trials as well as your triumphs. Nothing makes Him so real as to talk to Him about *everything*.

Reflection

Pause to consider Christ's love for you, how He desires to shape you and work out His plans for your life. In what ways has God used hardship to refine you?

The Value of Friendship

"A friend loves at all times."

PROVERBS 17:17

A friend is invaluable if we stumble or fall on the path of life. "Woe to him who is alone when he falls" (Eccl. 4:10). Let us watch out for each other's souls. If anyone is falling away from the truth or into some insidious trap, let us lift him up. Friendship ought to make our spirits glow. "How can one be warm alone?" (Eccl. 4:11). Of course, in a spiritual sense there are divine sources of warmth. The love of Christ kindles vehement heat. But it is certainly easier to keep up the temperature when we have a kindred heart beside us. Perhaps this was one reason why our Lord sent forth His disciples by two and two (see Luke 10:1).

A true friend makes us more able to withstand the Devil. It is a real help during the hour of trial to have a friend who will appropriate the words of our Lord, saying, "I have prayed for you, that your faith should not fail" (Luke 22:32). It is in God's design that His children should not journey alone. He made us to be companions, partners, and encouragers to one another.

Reflection

Why do you think it is part of God's plan for Christians to be partners and companions? Which friends have meant the most to you? How so?

Entrust Everything to God

"He guides them to their desired haven. Oh, that men would give thanks to the LORD for His goodness, and for His wonderful works to the children of men!"

PSALM 107:30–31

It is human nature to wish to obtain all we can from God and to give Him as little as possible of ourselves. We tend to fence off a part of ourselves for God, excluding Him from all the rest. But it is an arrangement that will not hold. Love will only give itself to love. The shadows of secrecy or reserve on either side will blight a friendship in which all the conditions seem perfectly adjusted. And many a life that might grow rich in its heritage of God is dwindled and marred because it sets a limitation on God's heritage of itself.

Give all you have to God. As He bought, so let Him possess, everything. He will occupy and keep you. He will bring fruit out of your rockiest nature, as the Norwegians raise crops on every scrap of soil on their mountain slopes. He will put into you the grace that you will give back to Him in fruit. He will win for Himself a great name as He turns your desert places into gardens and makes your wildernesses blossom as the rose.

Reflection

Why do we fence off parts of ourselves from God? What does He promise to do if we allow Him to guide us and thank Him for the good things He accomplishes in and through us?

The Value of Suffering

"Father, if it is Your will, remove this cup from Me; nevertheless not My will, but Yours, be done."

LUKE 22:42

Let all sufferers who read these lines go by themselves and dare to say the same words: "Not My will, but Yours." Say this thoughtfully and deliberately, not because you can *feel* it, but because you *will* it—not because the way of the cross is pleasant, but because it must be right. So you will be led to feel that all is right and well. A great calm will settle down on your heart, a peace that passes understanding.

In suffering and sorrow, God touches the minor chords, develops the passive virtues, and opens to view the treasures of darkness. Sorrow is a garden, the trees of which are laden with the fruits of righteousness; do not leave it without bringing them with you. Sorrow is a mine, the walls of which glisten with precious stones; do not retrace your steps into daylight without some treasure to carry on your way. Sorrow is a school; do not leave without learning lessons that will make you wise forever.

Reflection

How does God use sorrow to teach us valuable lessons? What have you learned from your suffering?

Broken Cisterns

"They have forsaken Me, the fountain of living waters, and hewn themselves cisterns—broken cisterns that can hold no water."

JEREMIAH 2:13

What an infinite mistake to miss the fountain freely flowing to quench our thirst and make our own cisterns, cracked and broken, in which are disappointment and despair. There is the cistern of *pleasure*, engraved with fruits and flowers, wrought at the cost of health and peace. There is the cistern of *wealth*, gilded and inlaid with costly gems. There is the cistern of *human love*, which, however fair and beautiful, can never satisfy the soul that rests in it alone. All these, constructed at infinite cost of time and strength, are treacherous and disappointing.

At our feet, the fountain of God's love is flowing through the channel of Jesus Christ, the Divine Man. He says to each of us, "Whoever drinks of the water that I shall give him will never thirst" (John 4:14). You who thirst for living, lasting refreshment, drink deeply of God's love and goodness. Forsake alliances, idolatries, and sins that have only left you parched. Open your heart that He may create in you the fountain of living water, leaping up to eternal life.

Reflection

How do the world's views of "cisterns" differ from God's view? Why do some people refuse to accept God's living water and keep trying to obtain their own?

Help Needy People

"Whoever has this world's goods, and sees his brother in need, and shuts up his heart from him, how does the love of God abide in him?"

1 JOHN 3:17

It is comparatively fruitless to give a meal here and there, without endeavoring, by practical sympathy and helping hand, to assist families by putting them in the way of helping themselves. To enable individuals or households to stand on their own feet and secure their own livelihood is immensely more important than to furnish temporary relief that supplies the need of today, but makes no permanent alteration in the circumstances of tomorrow or the future.

The ideal method of life is to use what you have to help others, to regard your possession of money as a stewardship for the welfare of the world. Instead of letting your clothes hang unused in the closet, give them to the respectable poor whose own are threadbare, that they may be able to occupy suitably the positions on which their livelihood depends. Whatever you have in the way of books, goods, spare rooms, elegantly furnished homes, view them all as so many opportunities of helping and blessing others.

Reflection

How might God want you to use your resources to help other people? Ask Him to bring you opportunities to bless others.

Give Your Anxieties to God

*"When you pray, go into your room, and when you have shut
your door, pray to your Father who is in the secret place."*

MATTHEW 6:6

How often we make no effort to be happy or to make the
best of things! We have had a bad night and have no scru-
ples about imposing our misery on a whole breakfast table of
people. We have anxiety gnawing at our heart, and we convey
the appearance of bearing a heavy burden. I suppose there is
in all of us a longing to be the object of friends' solicitude, and
there are times when we may freely unburden ourselves to get
advice and sympathy. But we have no right to add unduly to the
sorrows and anxieties of others, or to the travail of the world.

The life that is hidden with Christ in God is a very radiant
one because it hands over all its burdens and anxieties to the
Father in secret, and leaves them with Him. Thus it is "at
leisure from itself" to enter into the anxieties of others. The
reward of the person who lives with God in secret consists not
in thrones or crowns of gold, but in a growing sense of nearness,
affinity, and mutual understanding, which issue also in a growing likeness, though the saint does not know that his face shines.

Reflection

Are you radiant with the joy of the Lord? If not, why not?
What may be keeping you from turning over all your anxieties
to God?

God Exercises Restraint over Satan

"Does Job fear God for nothing? Have you not made a hedge around him?"

JOB 1:9–10

One of the profoundest studies in the Bible, the book of Job deals with the problem of evil. From first to last, the supreme questions in this wonderful piece of literature are: "Can God make man love Him for Himself alone and apart from His gifts?" And, "Why is evil permitted, and what part does it play in the nurture of the soul of man?"

The first chapter teems with helpful lessons. The anxiety of parents for their children should expend itself in ceaseless intercession on their behalf. The adversary is always on the watch, considering our conduct in order to accuse us before God, not only for overt sins but for unworthy motives. We cannot forget our Lord's words to Peter: "Satan has asked for you … but I have prayed for you, that your faith should not fail" (Luke 22:31–32). Christ never underestimated the power of Satan, the "prince of this world," but He is our great intercessor (see Heb. 4:14–16).

During circumstances of prosperity and happiness, we must never forget that it is God who plants a hedge about us, blesses our work, and increases our substance. It is not enough to endure our griefs sullenly or stoically. It should be our aim not only to hold fast to our integrity, but to trust God. There is a clue to the mystery of human life, which comes to the man who differentiates between the real and the unreal, the seen and the unseen.

Reflection

How can differentiating "between the real and the unreal, the seen and unseen" affect our view of God? In practical terms, what does it mean that God plants a hedge around us?

Strive for Unity in the Body of Christ

"[Bear] with one another in love, endeavoring to keep the unity of the Spirit in the bond of peace."

EPHESIANS 4:2–3

The unity or oneness of the Spirit is a divine reality that we don't have to make, only maintain. Try as we may, we can't make it one bit more perfect than it is. No bases of agreement, conferences, or conventions can do this. But we are called upon to give all diligence so that the divine ideal may be realized, as much as possible, among the saints.

There will never be uniformity, but there may be unity. The pipes in the great organ will never be all the same length or tone, but they may be supplied by the same breath and conspire to utter the same melody.

It must be our endeavor to guard against everything that would conflict with the inner unity of the Spirit. Jealousy, bickering, harsh words, uncharitable misrepresentations—these must be under the ban of the loving soul. It is often necessary to proclaim the truth, to defend it in the pulpit or drawing room, to enforce it to individuals to whom it may be extremely unpalatable. But love must prompt the speech and control the utterance. It is not enough to speak the truth; we must speak it in love.

Reflection

What roles do love and truth play in the unity of the body
of Christ? Why do we have to promote such unity diligently?

Recognize God's Power in Your Life

"[Know] the exceeding greatness of His power toward us who believe, according to the working of His mighty power."

EPHESIANS 1:19

God's power is *exceeding*, beyond our ability to conceive it. If we could only begin to comprehend—and access—God's power, everything about our lives would change for the better. We rise to heights untold.

Christian people constantly complain that they fall so far below their aspirations and hopes. They sigh at the foot of cliffs they cannot scale. But the fault is with themselves. We step into elevators that are attached to so many cables and levers—and we fully expect them to take us upward, never doubting that they will do so if we don't intentionally cause some malfunction. Likewise, if we keep in abiding fellowship with God—if we don't willfully step out of the range of His blessed help—we will find ourselves mounting with wings as eagles.

Reflection

Why is it vital for you to recognize the awesome power that's available to you through God? How does this truth influence the way you live?

Bring God's Peace to the World

"Blessed are the peacemakers."

MATTHEW 5:9

The strong emphasis that our Savior places on "peacemakers" indicates that the world is full of "peacebreakers." The world we live in is not naturally peaceful, and so God calls His children to intervene.

Is it not because men have lost the Fatherhood that they have lost the Brotherhood? The tender love of the father toward the child, and the father's love recognized *by* the child, is the great bond of security that instills and spreads peace. But since men have lost the consciousness of the love of God, they are consumed by the greed, lust, jealousy, hatred, and suspicion that are at the root of strife in the world. Therefore, God calls His children, with whom the bond has been restored, and says, "I desire that peace prevail over all discord and dissension. So I will send you forth, and your feet will be beautiful upon the mountains as you propagate peace." Since God desires that all of His children be peacemakers, let us heed that call.

Reflection

How seriously do you take God's call to be a peacemaker in the world? How, specifically, can Christians be peacemakers?

God Is with You Always

*"The mountains shall depart and the hills be removed,
but My kindness shall not depart from you."*

ISAIAH 54:10

M oses was an old man of eighty years. For forty years—the springtide of his life—he had basked in court favor. The son of the palace, though born in a slave hut. According to Stephen, he was renowned in deed and word, was eloquent in speech, learned in the highest culture of his age, accustomed to leading victorious armies in the field, and assisted in raising pyramids and treasured cities in peace. All that the ancient world could offer was at his feet (see Acts 7:22; Heb. 11:24–27). But this had been followed by forty other years of exile, poverty, and heartbreak. Instead of the riches of Egypt, he was engaged in tending the sheep of another, and the years slowly passed away in obscurity.

One afternoon a common thornbush suddenly seemed wrapped in flame. Then he heard that inner voice, familiar to all pure and humble hearts, that caused him to realize that the fire was no ordinary flame but the pledge and sign of God's presence.

We must not suppose that there was more of God in that common bush than in the surrounding landscape. It was simply the focusing of His presence that had always been there, as it is always everywhere. God is as near to each reader of these pages as He was to Moses at that moment. Take this to heart, you who are discouraged and downhearted. God comes to you, though you are humbled and scorched and at the end of yourself. He wraps around you, permeates you, and concentrates Himself on your need.

Reflection

If God is truly all around you, as close as He was to Moses by the burning bush, what difference should this truth make in your life? How can you know that God is with you always?

Five Tests Concerning Money

"The love of money is a root of all kinds of evil."
1 TIMOTHY 6:10

The fascination with money is one of the strongest in the world. There are five tests by which we may become aware whether this parasite is wrapping itself around us. Let us dare to question our hearts, and ask God to search them by His Holy Spirit.

First, do we find our mind going toward the little store of money that we have made, counting again and again its amount, and calculating how much more may be added in the course of another year?

Second, do we have a false sense of security due to our accumulated wealth? Over the years, has our dependence on God diminished as our accounts have grown? Do we look back on the days of early manhood and compare them with the present, feeling that we are becoming independent? Is our trust in God less complete than it used to be?

Third, do we envy other people who are making more money than we are, and do we consider ourselves inferior because we cannot keep pace?

Fourth, do we look at every service we perform and every new piece of information that we gather in the light of their monetary advantage?

Fifth, is it our habit to measure the gains of the year simply by what we have made with no reference to our spiritual growth? Is accomplishment gauged in terms of money accumulated rather than the good we have done?

We are wise to ask ourselves such questions as these reverently, because they will almost certainly reveal whether the absorbing love of money might be poisoning our heart and robbing it of its noblest attributes.

Reflection

What did you discover as you took this "test"? What changes might you need to make in action and attitude?

Christ's Resurrection Power

"Just as Christ was raised from the dead by the glory of the Father, even so we also should walk in newness of life."

ROMANS 6:4

The apostle tells us that we have union with the risen Christ. This changes everything about the way we view life and death, good and evil. Behind us lies the death of our Lord, which severed for His people their fellowship with the world. As the voice of praise or blame cannot reach the dead, so it is intended that the murmur of the world should not affect us, but that we should be set only on the will of God. We no longer focus on the *dying* but the *risen* side of the Savior's work. Behold Him as He goes forth on His upward way to the throne of glory. Seek to experience union with Him in the likeness of His resurrection.

Like the Israelites, we have passed from Egypt, never to return to it, and the Red Sea of Christ's redemption severs us from our former condition. We do not reckon ourselves to be dead to sin in the sense that our nature is now incapable of sinning. If we think thus, we shall soon be disillusioned and find that tendencies and strivings within us prove the contrary. But we must believe that we *have* died to sin, and whenever temptation comes, that it has no claim on us. Do not look at the tempter, but at Christ; instead, yield your eyes, ears, heart, and mind to Him, that He may make the best possible use of them.

Reflection

How should Christ's resurrection change our entire out-look on life? How should the fact that we have died to sin affect our daily lives?

Freedom through Christ

"For you were bought at a price; therefore glorify God in your body and in your spirit, which are God's."

1 CORINTHIANS 6:20

The fact that we have been bought at a price, not with corruptible things as silver or gold, but with the precious blood of Christ, lies at the foundation of all consecration (see 1 Peter 1:18). In consecration, we do not make ourselves Christ's, but recognize that we are His by an unalienable right. Among the Hebrews, an Israelite would sometimes sell himself into slavery until the year of Jubilee, or until one of his kinsmen redeemed him (see Lev. 25:47–50). Likewise, our kinsman, Christ, bought us back from sin, guilt, and condemnation. He says, as He buys us, "You will be for Me; you will not be for another."

Our Lord's claim on us is built on His supreme sacrifice. He "gave Himself for us," says the apostle Paul, "that He might redeem us from every lawless deed" (Titus 2:14). Oh, that we might keep this ever in mind, counting nothing as our exclusive possession but believing that all we have has been given to us to use in service to the Master.

Reflection

What does it mean to be consecrated to Jesus? In our culture, what things tend to hinder Christians from being completely faithful to God and serving Him fully?

Receiving the Holy Spirit

*"They were all filled with the Holy Spirit and began to speak
with other tongues, as the Spirit gave them utterance."*

ACTS 2:4

The majority of Christians have seemed to suppose that the
filling of the Holy Spirit was the prerogative of a few. They
have never thought of it as within their reach, and the church
has been paralyzed for lack of the only power that can avail in
the conflict against the world, the power that her ascending
Lord distinctly pledged. The Spirit was intended for *all* believers in Christ. How can we be filled up with the Spirit's power?
Consider:

We must desire to be filled for the glory of God. We must
seek the Spirit's power, not for our happiness and comfort, nor
even for the good that we may be better able to effect, but that
Christ may be magnified in our bodies, whether by life or death
(see Phil. 1:20).

We must bring cleansed vessels. God will not deposit His
precious gift in unclean receptacles. We must be washed in
the blood of Christ from all conscious filthiness and stain,
before we can presume to expect that God will give us what
we seek.

We must appropriate Him by faith. There is no need for
us to wait because the Holy Spirit has been given to the
church. We need not struggle and agonize in the vehemence

of entreaty, but simply have to take what God is waiting to impart. He gives the Holy Spirit to those who obey Him (see Acts 5:32).

We must be prepared to let the Holy Spirit do as He will with and through us. There must be no reserve, no holding back, no contrariety of purpose.

Reflection

In what ways are the points raised in this reading different from others you have heard? What would happen if Christians understood these truths—and met these simple conditions?

Jesus: The Son of God

"This is My beloved Son, in whom I am well pleased."

MATTHEW 3:17

God has many *sons*, but only one *Son*. When, on the morning of His resurrection, our Lord met the frightened women, He said, "I am ascending to My Father and your Father, and to My God and your God." But these words meant infinitely more of Himself than they could ever mean of man, however saintly or childlike. The word *Son* as used by our Lord and as understood by the Jews not only signified divine relationship, but also divine equality. Hence, on one occasion the Jews sought to kill Him, because He "said that God was His Father, making Himself equal with God" (John 5:18). And He, rather than correcting them, as He would have done had it been erroneous, went on to confirm and substantiate its truthfulness.

The impression Jesus of Nazareth left on all who knew Him was that of His extreme humility, but here was a point in which He could not diminish one bit, lest He should be false to His knowledge of Himself. And so Jesus died because He affirmed, amid the assumed horror of His judges, that He was the Christ, the Son of God.

Reflection

What is the significance to believers that Jesus is indeed the Son of God? Why do you think Jesus was so intent on demonstrating His humility as well as His authority as God's Son?

"Teach Us to Pray"

"In this manner, therefore, pray: Our Father in heaven, hallowed be Your name.... Give us this day our daily bread."

MATTHEW 6:9, 11

Our Lord was constantly praying to His Father. His disciples knew His habit of getting away for secret prayer, and they had on more than one occasion seen the transfiguring glory reflected on His face. Happy would it be for us if the glory of fellowship and communion with God were so apparent that men would come to us saying, "Teach us to pray" (Luke 11:1). Consider these thoughts on effective prayer:

Prayer must be simple. The Jewish proverb said, "Everyone who multiplies prayer is heard," but our Lord forbade senseless repetition by His teaching of the simple, direct, and intelligible petitions of the Lord's prayer.

Prayer must be reverent. The simplest utterances and closest intimacy will be welcomed and reciprocated by our Father in heaven. But we must remember that He is the great King, and His name is holy. Angels veil their faces in His presence. Approach Him with due reverence and respect.

Prayer must be unselfish. Our Lord so wove intercession into the structure of this prayer that none can use it without pleading for others. Though we will pray for our own needs and concerns, we should always realize that we are members of the body of Christ. The needs of others should fill our prayers too.

Prayer must deal with real needs. "Daily bread" implies every kind of need, and the fact that Jesus taught us to pray for it suggests that we may be sure that it is God's will to give.

Prayer must be in faith. We cannot but believe that we are as certain to prevail with God as the good man of the house with his friend, and if among men to ask is to get, how much more will we prevail with Him who loves us with more than a father's love (see Luke 11:9–13).

Reflection

How do these truths relate to your prayers? Are there some changes you need to make in your prayers?

An Audience of One

"Who is able to stand before this holy LORD God?"
1 SAMUEL 6:20

There is the general tendency to follow the practice of the majority. We drift with the current and allow our lives to be directed by our companions or the expectations of others. We make decisions according to public opinion.

What a revolution would come to us all if it became our one fixed aim and ambition *to stand before God* and always do those things that are pleasing in His sight—and His sight alone. What if every decision, every action, every word were determined solely on the basis of "standing before God"? Our lives would surely be radically altered.

All of us are aware of ties that hold us to the earth. We may discover what they are by considering what we cling to most—what we find hard to let go. Whatever it is, if it hinders us from living at the highest level, if it is a weight that impedes heavenward ascent, it should be laid deliberately on God's altar, that we may be able, that we live undiluted lives for Him.

Reflection

How might your life be different if your one aim is to stand before God and please Him? What does it mean to live an "undiluted" life for God?

Hold Nothing Back from God

"He poured [His Spirit] out on us abundantly through Jesus Christ our Savior, that ... we should become heirs according to the hope of eternal life."

TITUS 3:6–7

When traveling in Scotland, I met some farmers whose soil was naturally quite poor. Yet in answer to my inquiries, I found that they were able to raise crops of considerable weight and value. This seemed extraordinary to me. Out of nothing comes nothing is the usual rule. But they unraveled the mystery by telling me that they added, in enriching manure, all that they took out during the days of golden harvest.

Is not this the secret of any grace or wealth in our Christian lives? Not unto us, but unto You, God, be the glory! Whatever You do get out of us, You must first put in. And all the crops of golden grain, all the fruits of Christian grace, are Yours from us because You have—by Your blood and tears, by the sunshine of Your love and the rain of Your grace— enriched natures that in themselves were arid as the desert and barren as the sand.

We must see to it that we keep nothing back. There must be no reserve put on any part of our being. Spirit, soul, and body must be freely yielded to God.

Reflection

Are you fully committed to knowing God and obeying Him in all areas of life? What may be holding you back from yielding yourself completely to His cultivating care?

Receive God's Fullness

"In Him dwells all the fullness of the Godhead bodily."

COLOSSIANS 2:9

All the fullness of the Godhead dwells bodily in Christ, that we all might receive that fullness of Him, like streams of pure water continually replenishing wells and cisterns. In Him we have been made full in the purpose and intention of God, and in Him we may be made full by the daily reception of His grace, through the operation of the Holy Spirit.

There is not one, who is in Jesus by a living faith, who may not count on being filled by Him. As the lifeblood flows from the cistern-heart into each member and part of the body, so do the tides of life and love that emanate from the heart of Jesus pulse against the doors of all believing hearts. He fills all.

Reflection

What are some ways in which we try to create our own "cisterns" instead of finding complete fulfillment in Christ through the Holy Spirit? What does Christ long to do in each of our lives?

Be a Child of the Light

*"You were once darkness, but now you are light in
the Lord. Walk as children of light."*

EPHESIANS 5:8

When we live in communion with God—reflecting His love and goodness—we may be said to be walking in the light. And it is just in proportion as our steps tread the crystal pathway of light that our understanding becomes enlightened. In God's light, we see light. When the heart is pure, the eye is single focused. The opposite of this is also true. When we are alienated from the life of God, our understanding is darkened to His truth. The seat of infidelity is in the heart. Once a person becomes shut out from the life of God through the hardening of the heart, the light of the knowledge of the glory of God beats against a shuttered window, asking for admittance in vain.

If you would know God, you must resemble God. If you would learn God's secrets, you must walk with God. If you want to reflect God's light, you must live within His light. This means walking hand in hand with the Father every moment, every hour, every day.

Reflection

To what degree are you walking with God? What would allow you to better reflect His light?

Wear Your Armor into Battle

*"Put on the whole armor of God, that you may be able
to stand against the wiles of the devil."*

EPHESIANS 6:11

Each Christian will clash with the powers of hell, in his life and in his capacity as a soldier of the gospel of Christ. That Satan and his minions are called "the rulers of the darkness of this world" implies the fierce and protracted nature of this conflict that believers are called upon to engage in. There is no need, however, for us to shrink back, because through Christ's ascension all these principalities and powers were put under the feet of our Redeemer. When we abide in Him, we are more than a match for the mightiest forces of hell.

But the apostle makes it clear that we must possess certain personal qualities before we can avail ourselves of victory. This is the meaning of putting on the "whole armor" of God. Let us ponder this, for neglecting it has caused much of the failure of Christian workers. They are not careful enough concerning their personal character, so the Devil laughs at them. By their inconsistencies, they cut the sinews of their faith and disassociate themselves from the only source of victory that he dreads.

Reflection

What happens when we don't put on God's armor? Think about a time in your life when you didn't put it on and your personal character suffered as a result when Satan attacked you.

Live with Godly Integrity

*"We should live soberly, righteously,
and godly in the present age."*

TITUS 2:12

Of what use is it to speak of Jesus to those who are aware of some glaring inconsistency in our character? Can we declare God's holiness when our own attempts at holy living are tepid and feeble? The effect of our most eloquent entreaties is neutralized by our deeds, which speak loudest.

What a beautiful contrast there is between the laxity of too many of us and the scrupulous care of the apostle Paul. How watchfully he conducted himself as a representative for Christ. How sensitive he was to the least appearance of self-seeking. How gladly he went without what was in itself lawful, lest his ministry be compromised. Let each of us look upon Paul as an example and standard-bearer. Though he freely admitted his imperfections and weaknesses, he strived to live according to his high calling in Christ.

Reflection

In which areas of your life might anyone find fault with you? What are some practical examples of living with integrity?

Overcome Evil with Good

"Do not be overcome by evil, but overcome evil with good."
ROMANS 12:21

However men receive our testimony, whatever they may say and do against us, we must continue to be what our Lord calls us to be. We must let Him who is within us shine forth, so men must admit that it could be nothing but God's transforming grace that empowers us to live with such charity and goodness.

You ask what is the good of being good. Your oppressors vaunt themselves over you, take every advantage of your gentleness, and misinterpret your self-restraint. But it may be that your kindness is beginning to thaw the frozen soil in another's heart. The warmth emitted by your benevolence may, at first, seem to make no difference, but every hour of sunshine melts ice-covered souls a little bit more. Show kindness to all men, and trust God with the results.

Reflection

Why is it so hard to respond this way? What steps can we take to allow God to reflect His love through us when we interact with difficult people?

Receive the Blessedness of God

"Come, you blessed of My Father."
MATTHEW 25:34

Before Jesus came, men were content, happy, or mad with hilarious excitement, but not really *blessed*. This was a new word for the people, or it was an old word newly minted. They knew nothing of this deep, sweet secret of enjoying even in this world something of the very life of the deity. Only He who had come down from heaven knew of its existence or of the path that led to it.

God is significantly called "the blessed God." From all eternity, His vast and glorious nature has been as blessed as the vault of heaven seems full of ether. And Jesus came down from heaven to teach us this fact and make us understand our privilege. Since we have been made in God's likeness, we are each capable of a similar blessedness. One spirit with the Lord, we are privileged to share the very blessedness that fills His heart. Not in quantity but in quality, not in measure but in essence, that we may taste the blessedness of the blessed God.

Reflection

What does "blessedness" mean in your own words? Why is every Christian capable of sharing God's blessedness?

God's Unfolding Plan for You

*"Whatever you do in word or deed, do all in
the name of the Lord Jesus."*

COLOSSIANS 3:17

Nothing is more disastrous than aimless drift, for God
endows each person for a distinct purpose. Sometimes,
there may come a lucid moment when there flashes before us
a glimpse of the lifework for which we were sent forth. Still
other times, we may look ahead as into a veil of mist, and we
walk forward in faith, believing that the fog will lift.

Believe it: God will unfold our life purpose, if not in a flash
then step by gradual step. Let us go steadily forward, counting
on our Almighty Guide to supply the needed grace, wisdom,
and strength. He will not desert the work of His own hands!
What plan God has in mind for you, He will provide all to see
it through to completion.

Reflection

Why is it important for us to remember that God is unfold-
ing His will in each of our lives? How does God reveal His
plans and purposes for our lives?

The Riches of God

"According to the riches of His grace which He made to abound toward us in all wisdom and prudence."

EPHESIANS 1:7–8

We are all familiar with God's lavish abundance in nature. Every common hedgerow with its wealth of vegetation; every lazy trout stream, where the fish lie in the cool depths; every square foot of the midnight sky, set thick with rare jewels—these and countless other wonders attest the unsearchable resources of His power. But these are for all the world to see.

As the man of wealth opens richer stores to those who share his love than he displays to the casual visitor, so God has prepared for those who love Him things that eye has not seen, nor ear heard, nor the heart of man conceived (see 1 Cor. 2:9). There are riches of grace in the heart of God, of forgiveness and compassion and mercy, of which the foremost of the saints in the heavenly ranks, and the chief of sinners on Earth—however heavily they have drawn on them—know comparatively nothing. We have no standard for computing infinity, and infinity is the orbit in which God lives and loves.

Reflection

What riches of God's grace are you enjoying today? Thank Him for all that He has prepared for you.

Live by Faith in Christ

"The life which I now live in the flesh I live by faith in the Son of God."
GALATIANS 2:20

It is God's intention that we who believe should always live in Christ Jesus as the very foundation of our lives. In Him, we find our defense against the storm. In Him, we find shelter amidst howling winds. In Him, we find a sure mooring against the tempest.

Oh, to be always one of the faithful in Christ Jesus and to be able to say with the psalmist, "My goodness is nothing apart from You" (16:2). Then it would be easy at any moment to gain access with boldness into the presence of God, confident that what we asked for was according to His will. Then we should sit at His feet and be taught in Him. Then it would not always be so hard to give thanks for all things in His name. An artesian well, fed from heaven's deep joy, would then make perennial gladness in our hearts. Then we would never lack strength, our slender supply being fed from His almightiness on which we could draw perpetually.

Reflection

What does it mean to "live in Christ"? What blessings have you experienced from walking hand in hand with Him?

Blessed in All Circumstances

"Blessed are those who are persecuted for righteousness' sake,
for theirs is the kingdom of heaven."

MATTHEW 5:10

Blessedness is for us now and here. Not away in some distant world of bliss, where our circumstances will be entirely favorable and the mystery of sin and death ended, but in whatever situation we may be found at this present hour. Our real troubles are not in our circumstances, but in ourselves. If we had lived Paul's life, in our present state of heart, we should have known nothing of his rapturous experiences. If he could live in ours today, however tempest tossed and troubled, he would find in it elements of such exceeding rapture.

Jesus came to show that blessedness did not consist in our outward environment. Indeed, He distinctly taught that we might expect to suffer additional distresses for His and righteousness' sake. But He also taught that, if we possess a godly attitude and eternal perspective, we will be truly blessed. He said that blessedness is possible in the worst of circumstances, if only we will bear ourselves simply, bravely, truly, purely.

Reflection

How can a Christian be blessed in all circumstances—even the most challenging ones? Why doesn't blessedness consist in our outward environment?

Salvation Is for Everyone

*"Whoever drinks of the water that I shall give him will never thirst.
But the water that I shall give him will become in him a
fountain of water springing up into everlasting life."*

JOHN 4:14

I used to think that God had put His best gifts on a high shelf for us to reach up to them. I now find that the best are on the lower shelves, on the level of the nursery floor, that the babes may get them. There is a capacity for blessedness in each and all, just as there is a capacity for beauty, for love, for joy. The water of the well of Bethlehem was for David alone, but the water of the deep well of God's bliss, which our mighty Savior has won for us at awful cost, is for each poor outcast who comes, pitcher in hand, to take it freely.

There is no respect of persons with God. He does not exclude any; He welcomes all. Whoever you are, you are invited to this feast. Come, and enjoy the best God has to offer.

Reflection

What does it mean that "God's best gifts are on the lower shelves"? If each of us really realized what salvation really is, how might we live life differently?

Seek True Humility

"... showing all humility to all men."
TITUS 3:2

There are people (most objectionable, I think) who are always saying, "I am nothing and nobody." They insist on taking the backseats and declaring that they are not worth your notice. And yet you feel that they are as proud and desirous of the first places as those who in the Lord's parable took the best positions at the feast (see Luke 14:8–11). Indeed, this kind of false humility is more detestable than that which casts off all disguise. People sometimes act humbly because they are proud of a reputation for humility. They sit near the door so they might have the pleasure of being asked to the front.

Oh, for the humility that does not count itself humble! For the face that shines, and we know it not! For the quiet service that does not seek accolades!

To see true humility in action, we must turn to our blessed Lord, who, though rich, became poor (see 2 Cor. 8:9). No ambition lured Him forward, no fear held Him back, no desire to win power apart from the paths marked out by the Father was allowed to divert Him from the chosen track of obedience.

Reflection
What is true humility? In what ways did Jesus demonstrate it?

Don't Hold a Grudge

"If you bring your gift to the altar, and there remember that your brother has something against you, ... be reconciled to your brother, and then come and offer your gift."

MATTHEW 5:23–24

So often we are angry with people whom we have wronged. There is, therefore, no better way of saving us from explosions of anger than by undoing the wrong as soon as we become conscious of it in the clear light of God's presence. For this reason, our Lord bids us find out the brother whom we have wronged and make amends.

When reviewing events at the end of the day, we often become aware that we have, without saying as much, indicated to a brother ill feelings in a coldness of manner, change in behavior, or remote attitude. The symptom of our resentment toward him may have been slight but quite sufficient to convey displeasure. There is no more certain method of staying the progress of a tempest of anger than by at once becoming reconciled to the brother over that one small detail in which our antagonism has revealed itself.

Reflection

Why do we need to deal with even the smallest amount of anger properly? What can happen when we don't seek reconciliation and allow our anger to brew within us?

You Are Loved by the King

"That the God of our Lord Jesus Christ, the Father of glory,
may give to you the spirit of wisdom and
revelation in the knowledge of Him."

EPHESIANS 1:17

How often do we pause to consider the majesty and magnificence of God? Are we not apt to become so familiar with the thought of God as friend and companion (which He surely is) that we neglect to give Him praise for being King of kings and Lord of lords?

Remember that God loves you as no father ever loved the helpless baby given him from the dying hand of his young and cherished wife. Remember, too, His wealth as the Father of glory. This love for you, and this wealth bestowed upon you, is all the more overwhelming when you recognize the circumstances of this relationship: The God of the universe, the Creator of all, the King enthroned above the whole earth looks down upon you with favor, affection, and love everlasting.

Reflection

How often do you ponder God's majesty? What does it mean to you to know you're dearly loved by the King of kings?

Above All, Seek Him

*"Seek first the kingdom of God and His righteousness,
and all these things shall be added to you."*

MATTHEW 6:33

It is the object of God that His long-expected kingdom should come, that joyous life should replace death, and that love overcome hatred. In His great kindness, He has called us to help Him accomplish His high purpose, and He lays upon us a burden that we should not rest until the kingdom has come and His will is done on Earth as in heaven. For this we must labor and pray.

The contractor who has undertaken a railway line or the construction of a vast reservoir among the hills knows the necessity of providing for the well-being of the thousands of workers engaged with their spades or trowels. If they are to do work that will not disgrace him, he at least must see that their physical health and well-being are guaranteed. Is it likely, then, that God will be less careful and thoughtful of His own sons, whom He has called into fellowship with Him? Does He not know that we will do our best work when we are free from anxious care? Rest on this promise, which He gave: "All these things shall be added to you."

Reflection

Do you really believe this verse—and live accordingly? Why or why not? In what ways has God proven Himself faithful in the past?

Use the Shield of Faith

*"[Take] the shield of faith with which you will be able
to quench all the fiery darts of the wicked one."*

EPHESIANS 6:16

The Christian warrior must be vigorous in faith. As each fiery dart, tipped with the flames of hellish hate, comes speeding toward the soldier of the cross, he must catch and quench it on the golden shield of faith so it doesn't reach his head or heart. Sometimes a slander will be circulated for which you have given no occasion, or a venomous accusation will be hurled at you, or some horrible suggestion will be thrust between the joints of the armor. At the moment of such attacks, we are tempted to turn back and withdraw from the battle.

People will yield to the temptation if they are not sure they can enlist the help of the mighty Savior, who intercedes to cover our heads during the day of battle. But faith like this is only possible to him who has clean hands and a pure heart and who is living in daily fellowship with Jesus.

Reflection

How can we gain powerful faith to handle the challenges of life? If we really desire to exhibit vigorous faith, what kinds of things will Satan do to try to derail us?

Be Filled with the Holy Spirit

"And they were all filled with the Holy Spirit."

ACTS 2:4

Nothing can compensate the church or the individual Christian for the lack of the Holy Spirit. What the full stream is to the mill wheel, the Holy Spirit is to the church. We will stand powerless and abashed in the presence of our difficulties and foes until we learn what He can be, as a mighty tide of love and power in the hearts of His saints.

There are many people who are suffering from different forms of spiritual weakness, all of which are directly attributable to the lack of the Holy Spirit. Not that they are completely destitute of Him, because if they were they would not be Christians at all. But their spiritual power is at low ebb. This need not be, for the endowment of power and the baptism of fire are within reach. Let us be inspired with a holy ambition to get all that our God is willing to bestow.

We will experience joy untold and power unquenched if only we refuse to be satisfied with anything less than the full indwelling of the Holy Spirit.

Reflection

How do we refuse to be filled with the Spirit? Why do we sometimes not fully access His power?

A High Priest Who Loves Us

*"We have a great High Priest who has passed through
the heavens, Jesus the Son of God."*

HEBREWS 4:14

Jesus died because God loved us so much as to give Him up unto death for us all. God loved us from eternity, but before His love could have its blessed way with us, He needed to satisfy the claims of a broken law, to vindicate His righteousness, to be just. Therefore, He gave Himself to us in Jesus, who manifested God in the flesh, put away sin by the sacrifice of Himself, and entered in the Holiest of all to become a merciful High Priest. The only begotten and beloved Son is the reservoir in which the great love of God is stored.

It is a great comfort to know that God loved us when there was nothing to attract His love, because He will not be surprised by anything He discovers in us and will not turn from us at those manifestations of evil that sometimes make us lose heart. He knew the worst from the first. He did not love us because we were pure and untarnished, but to make us so. We cannot understand it, but since He began, He will not fail or become discouraged until He has finished His work.

Reflection

What does it mean to you that God "knew the worst from the first" and loved you still? Thank God today for His infinite love for you.

Becoming Poor in Spirit

"Blessed are the poor in spirit, for theirs is the kingdom of heaven."
MATTHEW 5:3

To be poor in spirit is to be vacant of self and waiting for God—to be emptied of self-reliance, to be thankfully dependent on the life-energy of the living God. The way to become poor in spirit is to realize that you have no power of your own by which to bless and help others, and then to open your whole being to the incoming and outflowing of the ever-blessed God.

Although Jesus was rich in all the divine fullness of His divine nature, He became poor and emptied Himself (see 2 Cor. 8:9). In other words, He determined not to speak His own words, follow His own scheme and plan, or work His mighty works in His own might. Rather, He became the channel and instrument through which His Father spoke, worked, and reconciled the world unto Himself. Let us, like Jesus, empty ourselves that we might be filled with God's mercy, power, and love.

Reflection

Are you poor in spirit? What does it mean to "empty yourself"?

Don't Lose Your Salt

———◆◇◆———

*"Salt is good; but if the salt has lost its flavor,
how shall it be seasoned?"*

LUKE 14:34

Salt left in contact with a damp soil loses its flavor and is good for nothing but to be trodden underfoot. So it is with Christians who lose their ability to "flavor" the world with goodness and righteousness. Lot is an example of this. Sodom went on its way, regardless of his presence in its midst. The Seven Churches of Asia lost their savor and with those of northern Africa were trodden down by Muslims. Nothing is so useless and worthless as an inconsistent and powerless Christian (see Ezek. 15:3–5).

What a comfort to know that our Shepherd restores the soul that is committed to His guardian care. If it turns aside into forbidden paths or drifts from Him, He goes after it and brings it home on His shoulder, rejoicing. He made Peter, in spite of his fall, a living witness to the truth, whom none of his enemies could gainsay or resist. It is His work by His Spirit to infuse the old flavor into savorless salt.

Reflection

How, specifically, are Christians called to be "salt"? Ask God to draw you close to Him and away from sin, that you might be full of flavor.

Blessedness Is for Today

"Blessed is he whose transgression is forgiven."
PSALM 32:1

There is a condition of soul, which the Master calls *blessedness*, that may be experienced and enjoyed by every person on Earth. Blessedness, first and foremost, comes from the forgiveness of sins and the acceptance of Christ as Lord and Savior. There is no soul of man so illiterate, so lonely, so poor in this world's goods, so beset with sins and overwhelmed by temptations that may not at this moment step into this life of blessedness. It is not necessary to ascend into heaven to bring the blessedness down or descend into the depth of the abyss to bring it up; it has not to be wrestled or wept for; it is not to be obtained by the merit of holy deeds or as the reward of devoted service.

We have not to do, feel, or suffer, but only to be. We acknowledge our utter dependence on God, our total need for Him and His forgiveness, and instantly blessedness begins.

Reflection

What blessings have you received because of God's forgiveness? Whom do you know who has not yet recognized the need for forgiveness? Pray for this person today.

Endeavor to Know God

*"I saw the Lord sitting on a throne, high and lifted up,
and the train of His robe filled the temple."*

ISAIAH 6:1

We live in troubled times. But always in human history, when outward events seem most distracting and distressing, God's servants are drawn into the secret place of the Most High. There we are shown the reassuring vision of God's overruling providence and might of His eternal reign.

When the land was passing through dark distress, and revolution was imminent, Isaiah beheld the stability of God's throne. It was "high and lifted up." The one man who was chosen out of all Israel to *see* was Isaiah. In all humility, he ascended the temple steps, hustled by crowds who went there as a mere religious form. Any of them appeared to need a revealing vision more than he did, but it was the man who had seen who now saw the Lord; it was the one saint in all Israel who appeared to be most in touch with God who was brought into still closer touch. The rest saw only the temple, the high altar, and the ritual, but *he* saw the "skirts of glory" filling every cranny of the holy place.

Let's not be satisfied with the outward and sensuous, with ritual however splendid, with sermons however magnificent! Those who are humble and persistent in their quest for God will hear notes other ears cannot catch and will enter the realm of the spirit that is closed to the outward observer. The world may be full of tumult; the floods have lifted up their voice, but the Lord on high is mighty. He will overcome, for through death, resurrection, and ascension He is Lord of lords and King of kings!

Reflection

How strongly do you desire to really *know* God? How, specifically, can you get to know Him better?

Subject Index

Scripture Index